Sociotechnical Insights and AI Driverless Cars

Practical Advances in Artificial Intelligence (AI) and Machine Learning

Dr. Lance B. Eliot, MBA, PhD

Disclaimer: This book is presented solely for educational and entertainment purposes. The author and publisher are not offering it as legal, accounting, or other professional services advice. The author and publisher make no representations or warranties of any kind and assume no liabilities of any kind with respect to the accuracy or completeness of the contents and specifically disclaim any implied warranties of merchantability or fitness of use for a particular purpose. Neither the author nor the publisher shall be held liable or responsible to any person or entity with respect to any loss or incidental or consequential damages caused, or alleged to have been caused, directly or indirectly, by the information or programs contained herein. Every company is different and the advice and strategies contained herein may not be suitable for your situation.

DEDICATION

To my incredible son, Michael, and my incredible daughter, Lauren.

Forest fortuna adiuvat (from the Latin; good fortune favors the brave).

CONTENTS

Acknowledgments iii

Introduction 1

Chapters

1 Eliot Framework for AI Self-Driving Cars 15

2 Start-ups and AI Self-Driving Cars 29

3 Code Obfuscation and AI Self-Driving Cars 45

4 Hyperlanes and AI Self-Driving Cars 59

5 Passenger Panic Inside an AI Self-Driving Car 73

6 Tech Stockholm Syndrome and Self-Driving Cars 89

7 Paralysis and AI Self-Driving Cars 103

8 Ugly Zones and AI Self-Driving Cars 119

9 Ridesharing and AI Self-Driving Cars 133

10 Multi-Party Privacy and AI Self-Driving Cars 147

11 Chaff Bugs and AI Self-Driving Cars 163

12 Social Reciprocity and AI Self-Driving Cars 177

13 Pet Mode and AI Self-Driving Cars 193

Appendix A: Teaching with this Material 207

Other Self-Driving Car Books by This Author 215

About the Author 239

Addendum 240

Lance B. Eliot

ACKNOWLEDGMENTS

I have been the beneficiary of advice and counsel by many friends, colleagues, family, investors, and many others. I want to thank everyone that has aided me throughout my career. I write from the heart and the head, having experienced first-hand what it means to have others around you that support you during the good times and the tough times.

To Warren Bennis, one of my doctoral advisors and ultimately a colleague, I offer my deepest thanks and appreciation, especially for his calm and insightful wisdom and support.

To Mark Stevens and his generous efforts toward funding and supporting the USC Stevens Center for Innovation.

To Lloyd Greif and the USC Lloyd Greif Center for Entrepreneurial Studies for their ongoing encouragement of founders and entrepreneurs.

To Peter Drucker, William Wang, Aaron Levie, Peter Kim, Jon Kraft, Cindy Crawford, Jenny Ming, Steve Milligan, Chis Underwood, Frank Gehry, Buzz Aldrin, Steve Forbes, Bill Thompson, Dave Dillon, Alan Fuerstman, Larry Ellison, Jim Sinegal, John Sperling, Mark Stevenson, Anand Nallathambi, Thomas Barrack, Jr., and many other innovators and leaders that I have met and gained mightily from doing so.

Thanks to Ed Trainor, Kevin Anderson, James Hickey, Wendell Jones, Ken Harris, DuWayne Peterson, Mike Brown, Jim Thornton, Abhi Beniwal, Al Biland, John Nomura, Eliot Weinman, John Desmond, and many others for their unwavering support during my career.

And most of all thanks as always to Lauren and Michael, for their ongoing support and for having seen me writing and heard much of this material during the many months involved in writing it. To their patience and willingness to listen.

Lance B. Eliot

INTRODUCTION

This is a book that provides the newest innovations and the latest Artificial Intelligence (AI) advances about the emerging nature of AI-based autonomous self-driving driverless cars. Via recent advances in Artificial Intelligence (AI) and Machine Learning (ML), we are nearing the day when vehicles can control themselves and will not require and nor rely upon human intervention to perform their driving tasks (or, that <u>allow</u> for human intervention, but only *require* human intervention in very limited ways).

Similar to my other related books, which I describe in a moment and list the chapters in the Appendix A of this book, I am particularly focused on those advances that pertain to self-driving cars. The phrase "autonomous vehicles" is often used to refer to any kind of vehicle, whether it is ground-based or in the air or sea, and whether it is a cargo hauling trailer truck or a conventional passenger car. Though the aspects described in this book are certainly applicable to all kinds of autonomous vehicles, I am focused more so here on cars.

Indeed, I am especially known for my role in aiding the advancement of self-driving cars, serving currently as the Executive Director of the Cybernetic Self-Driving Cars Institute.. In addition to writing software, designing and developing systems and software for self-driving cars, I also speak and write quite a bit about the topic. This book is a collection of some of my more advanced essays. For those of you that might have seen my essays posted elsewhere, I have updated them and integrated them into this book as one handy cohesive package.

You might be interested in companion books that I have written that provide additional key innovations and fundamentals about self-driving cars. Those books are entitled **"Introduction to Driverless Self-Driving Cars,"** **"Advances in AI and Autonomous Vehicles: Cybernetic Self-Driving Cars,"** **"Self-Driving Cars: "The Mother of All AI Projects,"** **"Innovation and Thought Leadership on Self-Driving Driverless Cars,"** **"New Advances in AI Autonomous Driverless Self-Driving Cars,"** and **"Autonomous Vehicle Driverless Self-Driving Cars and**

Artificial Intelligence" and "Transformative Artificial Intelligence Driverless Self-Driving Cars," and "Disruptive Artificial Intelligence and Driverless Self-Driving Cars, and "State-of-the-Art AI Driverless Self-Driving Cars," and "Top Trends in AI Self-Driving Cars," and "AI Innovations and Self-Driving Cars" and "Crucial Advances for AI Driverless Cars" (they are all available via Amazon). See Appendix A of this herein book to see a listing of the chapters covered in those three books.

For the introduction here to this book, I am going to borrow my introduction from those companion books, since it does a good job of laying out the landscape of self-driving cars and my overall viewpoints on the topic. The remainder of the book is all new material that does not appear in the companion books.

INTRODUCTION TO SELF-DRIVING CARS

This is a book about self-driving cars. Someday in the future, we'll all have self-driving cars and this book will perhaps seem antiquated, but right now, we are at the forefront of the self-driving car wave. Daily news bombards us with flashes of new announcements by one car maker or another and leaves the impression that within the next few weeks or maybe months that the self-driving car will be here. A casual non-technical reader would assume from these news flashes that in fact we must be on the cusp of a true self-driving car.

Here's a real news flash: We are still quite a distance from having a true self-driving car. It is years to go before we get there.

Why is that? Because a true self-driving car is akin to a moonshot. In the same manner that getting us to the moon was an incredible feat, likewise can it be said for achieving a true self-driving car. Anybody that suggests or even brashly states that the true self-driving car is nearly here should be viewed with great skepticism. Indeed, you'll see that I often tend to use the word "hogwash" or "crock" when I assess much of the decidedly *fake news* about self-driving cars. Those of us on the inside know that what is often reported to the outside is malarkey. Few of the insiders are willing to say so. I have no such hesitation.

Indeed, I've been writing a popular blog post about self-driving cars and hitting hard on those that try to wave their hands and pretend that we are on the imminent verge of true self-driving cars. For many years, I've been known as the AI Insider. Besides writing about AI, I also develop AI software. I do what I describe. It also gives me insights into what others that are doing AI are really doing versus what it is said they are doing.

Many faithful readers had asked me to pull together my insightful short essays and put them into another book, which you are now holding in your hands.

For those of you that have been reading my essays over the years, this collection not only puts them together into one handy package, I also updated the essays and added new material. For those of you that are new to the topic of self-driving cars and AI, I hope you find these essays approachable and informative. I also tend to have a writing style with a bit of a voice, and so you'll see that I am times have a wry sense of humor and also like to poke at conformity.

As a former professor and founder of an AI research lab, I for many years wrote in the formal language of academic writing. I published in referred journals and served as an editor for several AI journals. This writing here is not of the nature, and I have adopted a different and more informal style for these essays. That being said, I also do mention from time-to-time more rigorous material on AI and encourage you all to dig into those deeper and more formal materials if so interested.

I am also an AI practitioner. This means that I write AI software for a living. Currently, I head-up the Cybernetics Self-Driving Car Institute, where we are developing AI software for self-driving cars. I am excited to also report that my son, also a software engineer, heads-up our Cybernetics Self-Driving Car Lab. What I have helped to start, and for which he is an integral part, ultimately he will carry long into the future after I have retired. My daughter, a marketing whiz, also is integral to our efforts as head of our Marketing group. She too will carry forward the legacy now being formulated.

For those of you that are reading this book and have a penchant for writing code, you might consider taking a look at the open source code available for self-driving cars. This is a handy place to start learning how to develop AI for self-driving cars. There are also many new educational courses spring forth.

There is a growing body of those wanting to learn about and develop self-driving cars, and a growing body of colleges, labs, and other avenues by which you can learn about self-driving cars.

This book will provide a foundation of aspects that I think will get you ready for those kinds of more advanced training opportunities. If you've already taken those classes, you'll likely find these essays especially interesting as they offer a perspective that I am betting few other instructors or faculty offered to you. These are challenging essays that ask you to think beyond the conventional about self-driving cars.

THE MOTHER OF ALL AI PROJECTS

In June 2017, Apple CEO Tim Cook came out and finally admitted that Apple has been working on a self-driving car. As you'll see in my essays, Apple was enmeshed in secrecy about their self-driving car efforts. We have only been able to read the tea leaves and guess at what Apple has been up to. The notion of an iCar has been floating for quite a while, and self-driving engineers and researchers have been signing tight-lipped Non-Disclosure Agreements (NDA's) to work on projects at Apple that were as shrouded in mystery as any military invasion plans might be.

Tim Cook said something that many others in the Artificial Intelligence (AI) field have been saying, namely, the creation of a self-driving car has got to be the mother of all AI projects. In other words, it is in fact a tremendous moonshot for AI. If a self-driving car can be crafted and the AI works as we hope, it means that we have made incredible strides with AI and that therefore it opens many other worlds of potential breakthrough accomplishments that AI can solve.

Is this hyperbole? Am I just trying to make AI seem like a miracle worker and so provide self-aggrandizing statements for those of us writing the AI software for self-driving cars? No, it is not hyperbole. Developing a true self-driving car is really, really, really hard to do. Let me take a moment to explain why. As a side note, I realize that the Apple CEO is known for at times uttering hyperbole, and he had previously said for example that the year 2012 was "the mother of all years," and he had said that the release of iOS 10 was "the mother of all releases" – all of which does suggest he likes to use the handy "mother of" expression. But, I assure you, in terms of true self-driving cars, he has hit the nail on the head. For sure.

When you think about a moonshot and how we got to the moon, there are some identifiable characteristics and those same aspects can be applied to creating a true self-driving car. You'll notice that I keep putting the word "true" in front of the self-driving car expression. I do so because as per my essay about the various levels of self-driving cars, there are some self-driving cars that are only somewhat of a self-driving car. The somewhat versions are ones that require a human driver to be ready to intervene. In my view, that's not a true self-driving car. A true self-driving car is one that requires no human driver intervention at all. It is a car that can entirely undertake via automation the driving task without any human driver needed. This is the essence of what is known as a Level 5 self-driving car. We are currently at the Level 2 and Level 3 mark, and not yet at Level 5.

Getting to the moon involved aspects such as having big stretch goals, incremental progress, experimentation, innovation, and so on. Let's review how this applied to the moonshot of the bygone era, and how it applies to the self-driving car moonshot of today.

Big Stretch Goal

Trying to take a human and deliver the human to the moon, and bring them back, safely, was an extremely large stretch goal at the time. No one knew whether it could be done. The technology wasn't available yet. The cost was huge. The determination would need to be fierce. Etc. To reach a Level 5 self-driving car is going to be the same. It is a big stretch goal. We can readily get to the Level 3, and we are able to see the Level 4 just up ahead, but a Level 5 is still an unknown as to if it is doable. It should eventually be doable and in the same way that we thought we'd eventually get to the moon, but when it will occur is a different story.

Incremental Progress

Getting to the moon did not happen overnight in one fell swoop. It took years and years of incremental progress to get there. Likewise for self-driving cars. Google has famously been striving to get to the Level 5, and pretty much been willing to forgo dealing with the intervening levels, but most of the other self-driving car makers are doing the incremental route. Let's get a good Level 2 and a somewhat Level 3 going. Then, let's improve the Level 3 and get a somewhat Level 4 going. Then, let's improve the Level 4 and finally arrive at a Level 5. This seems to be the prevalent way that we are going to achieve the true self-driving car.

Experimentation

You likely know that there were various experiments involved in perfecting the approach and technology to get to the moon. As per making incremental progress, we first tried to see if we could get a rocket to go into space and safety return, then put a monkey in there, then with a human, then we went all the way to the moon but didn't land, and finally we arrived at the mission that actually landed on the moon. Self-driving cars are the same way. We are doing simulations of self-driving cars. We do testing of self-driving cars on private land under controlled situations. We do testing of self-driving cars on public roadways, often having to meet regulatory requirements including for example having an engineer or equivalent in the car to take over the controls if needed. And so on. Experiments big and small are needed to figure out what works and what doesn't.

Innovation

There are already some advances in AI that are allowing us to progress toward self-driving cars. We are going to need even more advances. Innovation in all aspects of technology are going to be required to achieve a true self-driving car. By no means do we already have everything in-hand that we need to get there. Expect new inventions and new approaches, new algorithms, etc.

Setbacks

Most of the pundits are avoiding talking about potential setbacks in the progress toward self-driving cars. Getting to the moon involved many setbacks, some of which you never have heard of and were buried at the time so as to not dampen enthusiasm and funding for getting to the moon. A recurring theme in many of my included essays is that there are going to be setbacks as we try to arrive at a true self-driving car. Take a deep breath and be ready. I just hope the setbacks don't completely stop progress. I am sure that it will cause progress to alter in a manner that we've not yet seen in the self-driving car field. I liken the self-driving car of today to the excitement everyone had for Uber when it first got going. Today, we have a different view of Uber and with each passing day there are more regulations to the ride sharing business and more concerns raised. The darling child only stays a darling until finally that child acts up. It will happen the same with self-driving cars.

SELF-DRIVING CARS CHALLENGES

But what exactly makes things so hard to have a true self-driving car, you might be asking. You have seen cruise control for years and years. You've lately seen cars that can do parallel parking. You've seen YouTube videos of Tesla drivers that put their hands out the window as their car zooms along the highway, and seen to therefore be in a self-driving car. Aren't we just needing to put a few more sensors onto a car and then we'll have in-hand a true self-driving car? Nope.

Consider for a moment the nature of the driving task. We don't just let anyone at any age drive a car. Worldwide, most countries won't license a driver until the age of 18, though many do allow a learner's permit at the age of 15 or 16. Some suggest that a younger age would be physically too small to reach the controls of the car. Though this might be the case, we could easily adjust the controls to allow for younger aged and thus smaller stature. It's not their physical size that matters. It's their cognitive development that matters.

To drive a car, you need to be able to reason about the car, what the car can and cannot do. You need to know how to operate the car. You need to know about how other cars on the road drive. You need to know what is allowed in driving such as speed limits and driving within marked lanes. You need to be able to react to situations and be able to avoid getting into accidents. You need to ascertain when to hit your brakes, when to steer clear of a pedestrian, and how to keep from ramming that motorcyclist that just cut you off.

Many of us had taken courses on driving. We studied about driving and took driver training. We had to take a test and pass it to be able to drive. The point being that though most adults take the driving task for granted, and we often "mindlessly" drive our cars, there is a significant amount of cognitive effort that goes into driving a car. After a while, it becomes second nature. You don't especially think about how you drive, you just do it. But, if you watch a novice driver, say a teenager learning to drive, you suddenly realize that there is a lot more complexity to it than we seem to realize.

Furthermore, driving is a very serious task. I recall when my daughter and son first learned to drive. They are both very conscientious people. They wanted to make sure that whatever they did, they did well, and that they did not harm anyone. Every day, when you get into a car, it is probably around 4,000 pounds of hefty metal and plastics (about two tons), and it is a lethal weapon. Think about it. You drive down the street in an object that weighs two tons and with the engine it can accelerate and ram into anything you want to hit. The damage a car can inflict is very scary. Both my children were surprised that they were being given the right to maneuver this monster of a beast that could cause tremendous harm entirely by merely letting go of the steering wheel for a moment or taking your eyes off the road.

In fact, in the United States alone there are about 30,000 deaths per year by auto accidents, which is around 100 per day. Given that there are about 263 million cars in the United States, I am actually more amazed that the number of fatalities is not a lot higher. During my morning commute, I look at all the thousands of cars on the freeway around me, and I think that if all of them decided to go zombie and drive in a crazy maniac way, there would be many people dead. Somehow, incredibly, each day, most people drive relatively safely. To me, that's a miracle right there. Getting millions and millions of people to be safe and sane when behind the wheel of a two ton mobile object, it's a feat that we as a society should admire with pride.

So, hopefully you are in agreement that the driving task requires a great deal of cognition. You don't' need to be especially smart to drive a car, and we've done quite a bit to make car driving viable for even the average dolt. There isn't an IQ test that you need to take to drive a car. If you can read and write, and pass a test, you pretty much can legally drive a car. There are of course some that drive a car and are not legally permitted to do so, plus there are private areas such as farms where drivers are young, but for public roadways in the United States, you can be generally of average intelligence (or less) and be able to legally drive.

This though makes it seem like the cognitive effort must not be much. If the cognitive effort was truly hard, wouldn't we only have Einstein's that could drive a car? We have made sure to keep the driving task as simple as we can, by making the controls easy and relatively standardized, and by having roads that are relatively standardized, and so on. It is as though Disneyland has put their Autopia into the real-world, by us all as a society agreeing that roads will be a certain way, and we'll all abide by the various rules of driving.

A modest cognitive task by a human is still something that stymies AI. You certainly know that AI has been able to beat chess players and be good at other kinds of games. This type of narrow cognition is not what car driving is about. Car driving is much wider. It requires knowledge about the world, which a chess playing AI system does not need to know. The cognitive aspects of driving are on the one hand seemingly simple, but at the same time require layer upon layer of knowledge about cars, people, roads, rules, and a myriad of other "common sense" aspects. We don't have any AI systems today that have that same kind of breadth and depth of awareness and knowledge.

As revealed in my essays, the self-driving car of today is using trickery to do particular tasks. It is all very narrow in operation. Plus, it currently assumes that a human driver is ready to intervene. It is like a child that we have taught to stack blocks, but we are needed to be right there in case the child stacks them too high and they begin to fall over. AI of today is brittle, it is narrow, and it does not approach the cognitive abilities of humans. This is why the true self-driving car is somewhere out in the future.

Another aspect to the driving task is that it is not solely a mind exercise. You do need to use your senses to drive. You use your eyes a vision sensors to see the road ahead. You vision capability is like a streaming video, which your brain needs to continually analyze as you drive. Where is the road? Is there a pedestrian in the way? Is there another car ahead of you? Your senses are relying a flood of info to your brain. Self-driving cars are trying to do the same, by using cameras, radar, ultrasound, and lasers. This is an attempt at mimicking how humans have senses and sensory apparatus.

Thus, the driving task is mental and physical. You use your senses, you use your arms and legs to manipulate the controls of the car, and you use your brain to assess the sensory info and direct your limbs to act upon the controls of the car. This all happens instantly. If you've ever perhaps gotten something in your eye and only had one eye available to drive with, you suddenly realize how dependent upon vision you are. If you have a broken foot with a cast, you suddenly realize how hard it is to control the brake pedal and the accelerator. If you've taken medication and your brain is maybe sluggish, you suddenly realize how much mental strain is required to drive a car.

An AI system that plays chess only needs to be focused on playing chess. The physical aspects aren't important because usually a human moves the chess pieces or the chessboard is shown on an electronic display. Using AI for a more life-and-death task such as analyzing MRI images of patients, this again does not require physical capabilities and instead is done by examining images of bits.

Driving a car is a true life-and-death task. It is a use of AI that can easily and at any moment produce death. For those colleagues of mine that are developing this AI, as am I, we need to keep in mind the somber aspects of this. We are producing software that will have in its virtual hands the lives of the occupants of the car, and the lives of those in other nearby cars, and the lives of nearby pedestrians, etc. Chess is not usually a life-or-death matter.

Driving is all around us. Cars are everywhere. Most of today's AI applications involve only a small number of people. Or, they are behind the scenes and we as humans have other recourse if the AI messes up. AI that is driving a car at 80 miles per hour on a highway had better not mess up. The consequences are grave. Multiply this by the number of cars, if we could put magically self-driving into every car in the USA, we'd have AI running in the 263 million cars. That's a lot of AI spread around. This is AI on a massive scale that we are not doing today and that offers both promise and potential peril.

There are some that want AI for self-driving cars because they envision a world without any car accidents. They envision a world in which there is no car congestion and all cars cooperate with each other. These are wonderful utopian visions.

They are also very misleading. The adoption of self-driving cars is going to be incremental and not overnight. We cannot economically just junk all existing cars. Nor are we going to be able to affordably retrofit existing cars. It is more likely that self-driving cars will be built into new cars and that over many years of gradual replacement of existing cars that we'll see the mix of self-driving cars become substantial in the real-world.

In these essays, I have tried to offer technological insights without being overly technical in my description, and also blended the business, societal, and economic aspects too. Technologists need to consider the non-technological impacts of what they do. Non-technologists should be aware of what is being developed.

We all need to work together to collectively be prepared for the enormous disruption and transformative aspects of true self-driving cars. We all need to be involved in this mother of all AI projects.

WHAT THIS BOOK PROVIDES

What does this book provide to you? It introduces many of the key elements about self-driving cars and does so with an AI based perspective. I weave together technical and non-technical aspects, readily going from being concerned about the cognitive capabilities of the driving task and how the technology is embodying this into self-driving cars, and in the next breath I discuss the societal and economic aspects.

They are all intertwined because that's the way reality is. You cannot separate out the technology per se, and instead must consider it within the milieu of what is being invented and innovated, and do so with a mindset towards the contemporary mores and culture that shape what we are doing and what we hope to do.

WHY THIS BOOK

I wrote this book to try and bring to the public view many aspects about self-driving cars that nobody seems to be discussing.

For business leaders that are either involved in making self-driving cars or that are going to leverage self-driving cars, I hope that this book will enlighten you as to the risks involved and ways in which you should be strategizing about how to deal with those risks.

For entrepreneurs, startups and other businesses that want to enter into the self-driving car market that is emerging, I hope this book sparks your interest in doing so, and provides some sense of what might be prudent to pursue.

For researchers that study self-driving cars, I hope this book spurs your interest in the risks and safety issues of self-driving cars, and also nudges you toward conducting research on those aspects.

For students in computer science or related disciplines, I hope this book will provide you with interesting and new ideas and material, for which you might conduct research or provide some career direction insights for you.

For AI companies and high-tech companies pursuing self-driving cars, this book will hopefully broaden your view beyond just the mere coding and development needed to make self-driving cars.

For all readers, I hope that you will find the material in this book to be stimulating. Some of it will be repetitive of things you already know. But I am pretty sure that you'll also find various eureka moments whereby you'll discover a new technique or approach that you had not earlier thought of. I am also betting that there will be material that forces you to rethink some of your current practices.

I am not saying you will suddenly have an epiphany and change what you are doing. I do think though that you will reconsider or perhaps revisit what you are doing.

For anyone choosing to use this book for teaching purposes, please take a look at my suggestions for doing so, as described in the Appendix. I have found the material handy in courses that I have taught, and likewise other faculty have told me that they have found the material handy, in some cases as extended readings and in other instances as a core part of their course (depending on the nature of the class).

In my writing for this book, I have tried carefully to blend both the practitioner and the academic styles of writing. It is not as dense as is typical academic journal writing, but at the same time offers depth by going into the nuances and trade-offs of various practices.

The word "deep" is in vogue today, meaning getting deeply into a subject or topic, and so is the word "unpack" which means to tease out the underlying aspects of a subject or topic. I have sought to offer material that addresses an issue or topic by going relatively deeply into it and make sure that it is well unpacked.

Finally, in any book about AI, it is difficult to use our everyday words without having some of them be misinterpreted. Specifically, it is easy to anthropomorphize AI. When I say that an AI system "knows" something, I do not want you to construe that the AI system has sentience and "knows" in the same way that humans do. They aren't that way, as yet. I have tried to use quotes around such words from time-to-time to emphasize that the words I am using should not be misinterpreted to ascribe true human intelligence to the AI systems that we know of today. If I used quotes around all such words, the book would be very difficult to read, and so I am doing so judiciously. Please keep that in mind as you read the material, thanks.

Lance B. Eliot

COMPANION BOOKS

If you find this material of interest, you might want to also see my other books on self-driving cars, entitled:

1. **"Introduction to Driverless Self-Driving Cars"** by Dr. Lance Eliot

2. **"Innovation and Thought Leadership on Self-Driving Driverless Cars"** by Dr. Lance Eliot

3. **"Advances in AI and Autonomous Vehicles: Cybernetic Self-Driving Cars"** by Dr. Lance Eliot

4. ***"Self-Driving Cars: The Mother of All AI Projects"*** by Dr. Lance Eliot

5. **"New Advances in AI Autonomous Driverless Self-Driving Cars"** by Dr. Lance Eliot

6. **"Autonomous Vehicle Driverless Self-Driving Cars and Artificial Intelligence"** by Dr. Lance Eliot and Michael B. Eliot

7. **"Transformative Artificial Intelligence Driverless Self-Driving Cars"** by Dr. Lance Eliot

8. **"Disruptive Artificial Intelligence and Driverless Self-Driving Cars"** by Dr. Lance Eliot

9. **"State-of-the-Art AI Driverless Self-Driving Cars"** by Dr. Lance Eliot

10. **"Top Trends in AI Self-Driving Cars"** by Dr. Lance Eliot

11. **"AI Innovations and Self-Driving Cars"** by Dr. Lance Eliot

12. **"Crucial Advances for AI Driverless Cars"** by Dr. Lance Eliot

13. **"Sociotechnical Insights and AI Driverless Cars"** by Dr. Lance Eliot.

All of the above books are available on Amazon and at other major global booksellers.

CHAPTER 1

ELIOT FRAMEWORK FOR AI SELF-DRIVING CARS

CHAPTER 1

ELIOT FRAMEWORK FOR AI SELF-DRIVING CARS

This chapter is a core foundational aspect for understanding AI self-driving cars and I have used this same chapter in several of my other books to introduce the reader to essential elements of this field. Once you've read this chapter, you'll be prepared to read the rest of the material since the foundational essence of the components of autonomous AI driverless self-driving cars will have been established for you.

When I give presentations about self-driving cars and teach classes on the topic, I have found it helpful to provide a framework around which the various key elements of self-driving cars can be understood and organized (see diagram at the end of this chapter). The framework needs to be simple enough to convey the overarching elements, but at the same time not so simple that it belies the true complexity of self-driving cars. As such, I am going to describe the framework here and try to offer in a thousand words (or more!) what the framework diagram itself intends to portray.

The core elements on the diagram are numbered for ease of reference. The numbering does not suggest any kind of prioritization of the elements. Each element is crucial. Each element has a purpose, and otherwise would not be included in the framework. For some self-driving cars, a particular element might be more important or somehow distinguished in comparison to other self-driving cars.

You could even use the framework to rate a particular self-driving car, doing so by gauging how well it performs in each of the elements of the framework. I will describe each of the elements, one at a time. After doing so, I'll discuss aspects that illustrate how the elements interact and perform during the overall effort of a self-driving car.

At the Cybernetic Self-Driving Car Institute, we use the framework to keep track of what we are working on, and how we are developing software that fills in what is needed to achieve Level 5 self-driving cars.

D-01: Sensor Capture

Let's start with the one element that often gets the most attention in the press about self-driving cars, namely, the sensory devices for a self-driving car.

On the framework, the box labeled as D-01 indicates "Sensor Capture" and refers to the processes of the self-driving car that involve collecting data from the myriad of sensors that are used for a self-driving car. The types of devices typically involved are listed, such as the use of mono cameras, stereo cameras, LIDAR devices, radar systems, ultrasonic devices, GPS, IMU, and so on.

These devices are tasked with obtaining data about the status of the self-driving car and the world around it. Some of the devices are continually providing updates, while others of the devices await an indication by the self-driving car that the device is supposed to collect data. The data might be first transformed in some fashion by the device itself, or it might instead be fed directly into the sensor capture as raw data. At that point, it might be up to the sensor capture processes to do transformations on the data. This all varies depending upon the nature of the devices being used and how the devices were designed and developed.

D-02: Sensor Fusion

Imagine that your eyeballs receive visual images, your nose receives odors, your ears receive sounds, and in essence each of your distinct sensory devices is getting some form of input. The input befits the nature of the device. Likewise, for a self-driving car, the cameras provide visual images, the radar returns radar reflections, and so on.

Each device provides the data as befits what the device does.

At some point, using the analogy to humans, you need to merge together what your eyes see, what your nose smells, what your ears hear, and piece it all together into a larger sense of what the world is all about and what is happening around you. Sensor fusion is the action of taking the singular aspects from each of the devices and putting them together into a larger puzzle.

Sensor fusion is a tough task. There are some devices that might not be working at the time of the sensor capture. Or, there might some devices that are unable to report well what they have detected. Again, using a human analogy, suppose you are in a dark room and so your eyes cannot see much. At that point, you might need to rely more so on your ears and what you hear. The same is true for a self-driving car. If the cameras are obscured due to snow and sleet, it might be that the radar can provide a greater indication of what the external conditions consist of.

In the case of a self-driving car, there can be a plethora of such sensory devices. Each is reporting what it can. Each might have its difficulties. Each might have its limitations, such as how far ahead it can detect an object. All of these limitations need to be considered during the sensor fusion task.

D-03: Virtual World Model

For humans, we presumably keep in our minds a model of the world around us when we are driving a car. In your mind, you know that the car is going at say 60 miles per hour and that you are on a freeway. You have a model in your mind that your car is surrounded by other cars, and that there are lanes to the freeway. Your model is not only based on what you can see, hear, etc., but also what you know about the nature of the world. You know that at any moment that car ahead of you can smash on its brakes, or the car behind you can ram into your car, or that the truck in the next lane might swerve into your lane.

The AI of the self-driving car needs to have a virtual world model, which it then keeps updated with whatever it is receiving from the sensor fusion, which received its input from the sensor capture and the sensory devices.

D-04: System Action Plan

By having a virtual world model, the AI of the self-driving car is able to keep track of where the car is and what is happening around the car. In addition, the AI needs to determine what to do next. Should the self-driving car hit its brakes? Should the self-driving car stay in its lane or swerve into the lane to the left? Should the self-driving car accelerate or slow down?

A system action plan needs to be prepared by the AI of the self-driving car. The action plan specifies what actions should be taken. The actions need to pertain to the status of the virtual world model. Plus, the actions need to be realizable.

This realizability means that the AI cannot just assert that the self-driving car should suddenly sprout wings and fly. Instead, the AI must be bound by whatever the self-driving car can actually do, such as coming to a halt in a distance of X feet at a speed of Y miles per hour, rather than perhaps asserting that the self-driving car come to a halt in 0 feet as though it could instantaneously come to a stop while it is in motion.

D-05: Controls Activation

The system action plan is implemented by activating the controls of the car to act according to what the plan stipulates. This might mean that the accelerator control is commanded to increase the speed of the car. Or, the steering control is commanded to turn the steering wheel 30 degrees to the left or right.

One question arises as to whether or not the controls respond as they are commanded to do. In other words, suppose the AI has commanded the accelerator to increase, but for some reason it does not do so. Or, maybe it tries to do so, but the speed of the car does not increase. The controls activation feeds back into the virtual world model, and simultaneously the virtual world model is getting updated from the sensors, the sensor capture, and the sensor fusion. This allows the AI to ascertain what has taken place as a result of the controls being commanded to take some kind of action.

By the way, please keep in mind that though the diagram seems to have a linear progression to it, the reality is that these are all aspects of the self-driving car that are happening in parallel and simultaneously. The sensors are capturing data, meanwhile the sensor fusion is taking place, meanwhile the virtual model is being updated, meanwhile the system action plan is being formulated and reformulated, meanwhile the controls are being activated.

This is the same as a human being that is driving a car. They are eyeballing the road, meanwhile they are fusing in their mind the sights, sounds, etc., meanwhile their mind is updating their model of the world around them, meanwhile they are formulating an action plan of what to do, and meanwhile they are pushing their foot onto the pedals and steering the car. In the normal course of driving a car, you are doing all of these at once. I mention this so that when you look at the diagram, you will think of the boxes as processes that are all happening at the same time, and not as though only one happens and then the next.

They are shown diagrammatically in a simplistic manner to help comprehend what is taking place. You though should also realize that they are working in parallel and simultaneous with each other. This is a tough aspect in that the inter-element communications involve latency and other aspects that must be taken into account. There can be delays in one element updating and then sharing its latest status with other elements.

D-06: Automobile & CAN

Contemporary cars use various automotive electronics and a Controller Area Network (CAN) to serve as the components that underlie the driving aspects of a car. There are Electronic Control Units (ECU's) which control subsystems of the car, such as the engine, the brakes, the doors, the windows, and so on.

The elements D-01, D-02, D-03, D-04, D-05 are layered on top of the D-06, and must be aware of the nature of what the D-06 is able to do and not do.

D-07: In-Car Commands

Humans are going to be occupants in self-driving cars. In a Level 5 self-driving car, there must be some form of communication that takes place between the humans and the self-driving car. For example, I go into a self-driving car and tell it that I want to be driven over to Disneyland, and along the way I want to stop at In-and-Out Burger. The self-driving car now parses what I've said and tries to then establish a means to carry out my wishes.

In-car commands can happen at any time during a driving journey. Though my example was about an in-car command when I first got into my self-driving car, it could be that while the self-driving car is carrying out the journey that I change my mind. Perhaps after getting stuck in traffic, I tell the self-driving car to forget about getting the burgers and just head straight over to the theme park. The self-driving car needs to be alert to in-car commands throughout the journey.

D-08: VX2 Communications

We will ultimately have self-driving cars communicating with each other, doing so via V2V (Vehicle-to-Vehicle) communications. We will also have self-driving cars that communicate with the roadways and other aspects of the transportation infrastructure, doing so via V2I (Vehicle-to-Infrastructure).

The variety of ways in which a self-driving car will be communicating with other cars and infrastructure is being called V2X, whereby the letter X means whatever else we identify as something that a car should or would want to communicate with. The V2X communications will be taking place simultaneous with everything else on the diagram, and those other elements will need to incorporate whatever it gleans from those V2X communications.

D-09: Deep Learning

The use of Deep Learning permeates all other aspects of the self-driving car. The AI of the self-driving car will be using deep learning to do a better job at the systems action plan, and at the controls activation, and at the sensor fusion, and so on.

Currently, the use of artificial neural networks is the most prevalent form of deep learning. Based on large swaths of data, the neural networks attempt to "learn" from the data and therefore direct the efforts of the self-driving car accordingly.

D-10: Tactical AI

Tactical AI is the element of dealing with the moment-to-moment driving of the self-driving car. Is the self-driving car staying in its lane of the freeway? Is the car responding appropriately to the controls commands? Are the sensory devices working?

For human drivers, the tactical equivalent can be seen when you watch a novice driver such as a teenager that is first driving. They are focused on the mechanics of the driving task, keeping their eye on the road while also trying to properly control the car.

D-11: Strategic AI

The Strategic AI aspects of a self-driving car are dealing with the larger picture of what the self-driving car is trying to do. If I had asked that the self-driving car take me to Disneyland, there is an overall journey map that needs to be kept and maintained.

There is an interaction between the Strategic AI and the Tactical AI. The Strategic AI is wanting to keep on the mission of the driving, while the Tactical AI is focused on the particulars underway in the driving effort. If the Tactical AI seems to wander away from the overarching mission, the Strategic AI wants to see why and get things back on track. If the Tactical AI realizes that there is something amiss on the self-driving car, it needs to alert the Strategic AI accordingly and have an adjustment to the overarching mission that is underway.

D-12: Self-Aware AI

Very few of the self-driving cars being developed are including a Self-Aware AI element, which we at the Cybernetic Self-Driving Car Institute believe is crucial to Level 5 self-driving cars.

The Self-Aware AI element is intended to watch over itself, in the sense that the AI is making sure that the AI is working as intended. Suppose you had a human driving a car, and they were starting to drive erratically. Hopefully, their own self-awareness would make them realize they themselves are driving poorly, such as perhaps starting to fall asleep after having been driving for hours on end. If you had a passenger in the car, they might be able to alert the driver if the driver is starting to do something amiss. This is exactly what the Self-Aware

AI element tries to do, it becomes the overseer of the AI, and tries to detect when the AI has become faulty or confused, and then find ways to overcome the issue.

D-13: Economic

The economic aspects of a self-driving car are not per se a technology aspect of a self-driving car, but the economics do indeed impact the nature of a self-driving car. For example, the cost of outfitting a self-driving car with every kind of possible sensory device is prohibitive, and so choices need to be made about which devices are used. And, for those sensory devices chosen, whether they would have a full set of features or a more limited set of features.

We are going to have self-driving cars that are at the low-end of a consumer cost point, and others at the high-end of a consumer cost point. You cannot expect that the self-driving car at the low-end is going to be as robust as the one at the high-end. I realize that many of the self-driving car pundits are acting as though all self-driving cars will be the same, but they won't be. Just like anything else, we are going to have self-driving cars that have a range of capabilities. Some will be better than others. Some will be safer than others. This is the way of the real-world, and so we need to be thinking about the economics aspects when considering the nature of self-driving cars.

D-14: Societal

This component encompasses the societal aspects of AI which also impacts the technology of self-driving cars. For example, the famous Trolley Problem involves what choices should a self-driving car make when faced with life-and-death matters. If the self-driving car is about to either hit a child standing in the roadway, or instead ram into a tree at the side of the road and possibly kill the humans in the self-driving car, which choice should be made?

We need to keep in mind the societal aspects will underlie the AI of the self-driving car. Whether we are aware of it explicitly or not, the AI will have embedded into it various societal assumptions.

D-15: Innovation

I included the notion of innovation into the framework because we can anticipate that whatever a self-driving car consists of, it will continue to be innovated over time. The self-driving cars coming out in the next several years will undoubtedly be different and less innovative than the versions that come out in ten years hence, and so on.

Framework Overall

For those of you that want to learn about self-driving cars, you can potentially pick a particular element and become specialized in that aspect. Some engineers are focusing on the sensory devices. Some engineers focus on the controls activation. And so on. There are specialties in each of the elements.

Researchers are likewise specializing in various aspects. For example, there are researchers that are using Deep Learning to see how best it can be used for sensor fusion. There are other researchers that are using Deep Learning to derive good System Action Plans. Some are studying how to develop AI for the Strategic aspects of the driving task, while others are focused on the Tactical aspects.

A well-prepared all-around software developer that is involved in self-driving cars should be familiar with all of the elements, at least to the degree that they know what each element does. This is important since whatever piece of the pie that the software developer works on, they need to be knowledgeable about what the other elements are doing.

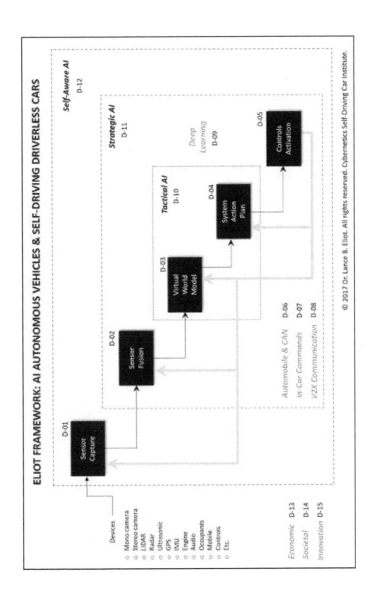

ELIOT FRAMEWORK: AI AUTONOMOUS VEHICLES & SELF-DRIVING DRIVERLESS CARS

CHAPTER 2

START-UPS AND
AI SELF-DRIVING CARS

CHAPTER 2

START-UPS AND
AI SELF-DRIVING CARS

Hear ye, hear ye! Start-up's, start your engines. There's a bonanza of AI self-driving car start-ups and likely many more soon to be birthed. It's a sensible thing to consider, given the pot of gold at the end of the rainbow. There are predictions that the self-driving car market will be around $20 billion by 2024, $800 billion by 2035, and perhaps $7 trillion by 2050. It's a big money opportunity.

For those of you that say you aren't only about the money, there's also the chance that you can aid in the emergence of something that is anticipated to radically change society as we know it today. There is the added benefit that it could save lives. AI self-driving cars are anticipated to have a slew of beneficial outcomes and thus you can either seek to make your mark on the world or go for the dough, or try to do both at the same time (a twofer!).

In working with and for various Venture Capital (VC) and Private Equity (PE) firms, I know well what is considered viable and investment-worthy start-up's in the AI self-driving cars realm. In addition, I'm an angel investor and incubator mentor, and perhaps most importantly herein for today's discussion, I'm a frequent pitch judge at start-up pitches, especially in Silicon Valley (Northern California) and in Silicon Beach (Southern California).

For those of you that are budding entrepreneurs, I want to offer some sage advice about what kind of start-ups are being sought and also how to best pitch your start-up.

At the Cybernetic AI Self-Driving Car Institute, we are developing AI software for self-driving cars, and we are fostering the emergence and growth of fellow start-ups in this space.

I've had some entrepreneurs say to me they aren't sure what the potential product sphere of AI self-driving cars consist of. They are raring to go in terms of applying their AI skills, but don't know where to aim their skills at. That's a question easily answered.

First step, take a look at my framework for AI self-driving cars (see Chapter 1).

You will need to identify some aspect as based on the framework that will be the niche of your start-up. In fact, when a start-up approaches me and says they are in the AI self-driving car space, I ask them where they fit within the framework. It's an easy and quick way to position yourself. Otherwise, it takes a lot of verbal jujitsu to try and explain what you are aiming to do.

For most VC/PE's, they want the short-and-sweet indication of what you do. If you can't say it in one sentence, you've lost a ton of potential VC/PE's and they'll quickly move along to someone else that can succinctly say what they do.

For example, per the framework, these are the five of the key aspects of AI self-driving cars:

D-01: Sensor Capture
D-02: Sensor Fusion
D-03: Virtual World Model
D-04: AI Action Plan
D-05: Car Controls Activation

If you have come up with a tremendously new way to compress camera images, which you believe could revolutionize the ability of AI self-driving cars to readily cope with the voluminous data being captured by the cameras of a self-driving car, I'd say that you are squarely in D-01 "Sensor Capture" of the framework.

This is handy for purposes of saying what you are doing, and also for implying what you are not doing. Since in this case you are saying you are doing the D-01 of Sensor Capture, it also by silent implication says you aren't doing D-05 Car Controls Activation or any of the other areas of the framework. For potential investors, they need to assess whether you are in an area of interest to them. If your niche is muddied, it will create confusion for those investors and they'll likely walk on.

Now, this doesn't suggest you can't be in more than one area or niche. You can be. One might say that the auto firms like Tesla are in the entire framework. Same might be said for Google's Waymo, a tech firm, not an auto firm, but that is striving to become a king of the AI self-driving car.

For most start-up's, I'd assert that trying to claim you encompass the entire framework is a bit ambitious and likely to be viewed with a strong dose of skepticism by most investors.

You'll likely hear that investors are typically looking for someone that wants to swing for the fences. This is true and means that they tend to prefer someone with a big vision that will layout an aim that is ambitious. Investors want to put money into something that has a huge upside potential. If they think your niche is too narrow and won't make much money ultimately, it's just not worth their risk or time, especially if they can find someone else that has such a vision.

At the same time, a vision that is farfetched will likely get you placed into the oddball category. There's always at these pitch competitions someone that says they have come up with a new kind of car that will replace all other cars ever invented or conceived. My Spiderman tingling sense usually right away gets suspicious.

One of my "favorite" wild claims was the pitch that said all AI of today is like child's play and he had invented a new kind of AI that surpasses all other AI's. When I tried to probe as to what this magical new AI might be, he refused to say and said that only an investor that put up at least $1 million dollars would get a chance to peek at what he has. Serious or scam? Crazy or wily as a fox?

That being said, often the source of an initial investment in your start-up is via the so-called "FFF" which stands for Family, Friends, or Fools. The last of those three F's, Fools, refers to people that sometimes put their life savings or their college fund into a speculative start-up and don't have any clue as to what they are doing. I believe that the pitch about the "new kind of AI" was aiming toward that third F (I asked him too whether any Family or Friends had yet invested in his startup, and the answer was no, which I think says enough right there about his wacky claim).

If you aren't sure what area of the framework you could best contribute toward in terms of doing a start-up on the matter, you should consider researching more so what's happening in the AI self-driving car industry.

For example, I've predicted that the Internet of Things (IoT) will be a significant allied emergent technology to AI self-driving cars. Thus, if you are already versed in IoT, you can consider shaping your IoT expertise into an AI self-driving cars niche. Another hot high-tech is blockchain. If you have expertise in blockchain, consider applying it to AI self-driving cars.

Decide Whether to Focus on the Core or on the Edge

You might also consider whether you are most interested and suited for a main "core" aspect of AI self-driving cars, or whether you'd aim at an "edge" part of the AI self-driving cars space. The edge of any problem area is considered something not necessarily prime or at the core of the matter, and instead something that is secondary. For a start-up, you don't need to be at the core of the AI self-driving car space.

There are numerous secondary or edge problems that are emerging and will ultimately have great potential and value.

The upside for picking an edge problem is that there are likely less competitors duking it out in that space. You have a chance to be the first, or at least be able to stand out among what otherwise will potentially be other small competitors. If you pick a core topic, the odds are that the big guns are already pursuing the matter. Those big guns are large auto firms and tech firms in the AI self-driving car space. They have more money than you, and can readily possibly surpass whatever you can come up with. That being said, often times the big firm's mess-up trying to do something core, perhaps due to their own bureaucratic ways or some other internal snarl, and so there is a chance you could solve something they cannot.

If you pick an edge problem, it often means that there are less understood ways of solving it and so you'll have a higher burden of proof that you have indeed found a means to solve it. What makes you so special that you found a solution that no one else has? Is what you've come up with even practical?

The other difficulty can be finding an investor that sees the edge problem as something worthy of attention, especially so in the near-term. I say this because suppose your edge problem won't really blossom in the marketplace until let's say the year 2030. That implies that an investor needs to pump money into something that they presumably won't see much return until a decade from now. Few investors have that kind of time horizon in mind. Most have a much shorter time horizon for which they want to cash out, and so want to see whatever you've got come to fruition in the next few years, and not wait for a decade or more.

This then brings us to the ways in which you should be putting together your start-up and also how therefore you'll want to pitch it.

I show herein a handy diagram from my book on "How to Win a Startup Pitch Competition: Successful Insights from a Topnotch Judge for Boosting Your Startup" by Lance Eliot, available on Amazon and at other booksellers. See https://www.amazon.com/How-Win-Startup-Pitch-Competition/dp/0692793933

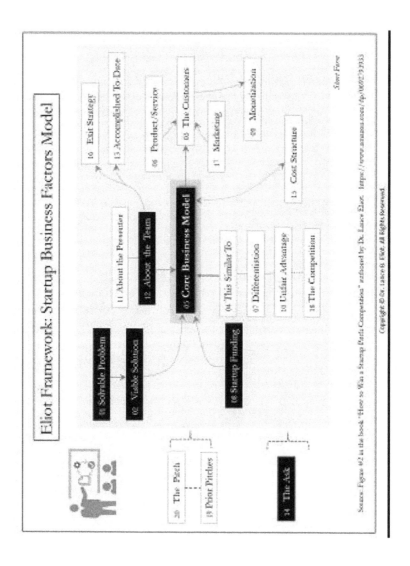

Here's your most important tip about your start-up and also about pitch competitions – *you need to be able to articulate what your start-up is about regarding each of the 20 factors listed.*

The reason I mention this is because many if not most entrepreneurs only consider a handful of the factors, and then they get stuck because they weren't considering the full range of factors. They get stuck in the sense that their start-up doesn't get off the ground. They get stuck in the sense that when they pitch to investors they get fried and peppered with questions about their start-up that they cannot answer. Don't be one of those kinds of entrepreneurs. Don't be one of those kinds of most-likely-to-fail start-ups.

Time and again, I serve as a judge at pitch competitions and the pitches are inadequate. It's not necessarily because the person wasn't a good speaker, which is the aspect that many entrepreneurs worry about and assume will get them dinged the most. I assure you that most of my fellow judges know that high-tech entrepreneurs are bound to be mediocre speakers. We accept that fact. It's acceptable as long as the entrepreneurs can otherwise address the 20 factors.

A savvy pitch judge and investor looks to see whether the high-tech entrepreneur has seriously thought about what they are doing. Has the entrepreneur just jumbled together some ideas, or have they really considered what it takes to make something into a business?

If you seem to have written something on the back of the napkin, and you've put no other effort into your start-up, it leaves a bad impression. And so unless you really have discovered how to create a perpetual motion machine or have a Noble Prize invention, you'll need to be ready to showcase the full gamut of considerations.

Let's briefly walk through the factors herein (more details are available in the book).

01 Solvable Problem
02 Viable Solution
03 The Customers
04 This Similar To
05 Core Business Model
06 Product/Service
07 Differentiation
08 Startup Funding
09 Monetization
10 Unfair Advantage
11 About the Presenter
12 About the Team
13 Accomplished To-Date
14 The Ask
15 Cost Structure
16 Exit Strategy
17 Marketing
18 The Competition
19 Prior Pitches
20 The Pitch

These are numbered for ease of reference, rather than due to priority. The ones shown in the diagram as darkened are the key six that you need to make sure you cover in any pitch. Sometimes for a pitch they do super-fast rounds like speed dating, and you get only 30 seconds to say something, in which case, cover at least the key six. Believe it or not, a standard pitch competition is about 3-4 minutes for the pitch and you can actually cover all 20 factors if you know how to do so.

Indeed, what usually happens at a pitch competition is that if you fail to cover all of the 20 factors, the judges are likely to pound at you about those omitted aspects during the Q&A portion. If you want to avoid those kind of crushing blows, cover the full set of 20. This will then cause the judges to perhaps dig more deeply into a particular area already covered, but at least it means that they won't attack you about the aspect that you left out something crucial.

Here's an even scarier secret that most entrepreneurs don't realize about their pitches – if you omit something crucial, and if the judges don't have time available to ask you about the topic, many judges will assume that you are "clueless" and don't even know that you omitted a crucial factor. This makes them queasy as it implies you haven't done your homework and you aren't really serious about your startup. Just thought you'd like to know.

Well, let's start with the how you usually should begin, in terms of both what you start-up is about and also how you should pitch it, namely what is the problem that you are trying to solve?

Notice that it's entitled "Solvable Problem" and shown labeled as item #1. I admit that even though the list of factors is not necessarily in sequence of priority, as mentioned earlier, I did nonetheless purposely put the nature of the problem at the beginning of the list. This is vital as a factor. You need to be able to explain that your start-up is going to solve some kind of problem. Furthermore, it needs to be a solvable problem.

I've seen several start-ups that said they were aiming to provide common sense reasoning for AI self-driving cars. I think we can agree that common sense reasoning is really more of a solution than it is a problem. Thus, they were telling me the solution, rather than the problem to be solved. When I asked them what good would it do for an AI self-driving car to embody common sense reasoning, they explained that it would enable the AI to drive the car in a manner more akin to how humans drive a car.

I then pointed out that if that's the case, they are then trying to solve a problem consisting of trying to get AI to be able to drive cars more like humans do. Of the myriad of ways to solve that problem, they have chosen to develop common sense reasoning. Therefore, they should begin by indicating that there is a problem that AI cannot yet achieve true self-driving because it lacks common sense, that's the pain point, and they are asserting that a means to solve this problem is to develop software that embodies common sense reasoning.

Do you see the important distinction there? They had a hard time seeing it.

Notice that this also intertwines the factor 01 and the factor 02, namely that your start-up should have a relatively crisp Solvable Problem and a relatively crisp Viable Solution.

Let's consider these two peas in a pod, the solvable problem and the viable solution.

If the problem is that self-driving cars cannot climb up walls, I'd wonder right away whether this is a solvable problem or not. Is it feasible to make a car that climbs up walls? I've not seen one as yet, and maybe it is possible, but it verges right now on the unsolvable side of things. If you say that the problem is lack of common sense reasoning, it seems like it is potentially solvable in that there is a lot of ongoing work on trying to achieve common sense reasoning capabilities in AI. I'd believe that this can be a solvable problem (though, not everyone would agree with me on this point, and some believe we won't ever be able to produce common sense reasoning – sad face!).

Investors are leery of an unsolvable problem since they figure investing in trying to solve it is going to either never lead to a solution or be a long time and costly to get there. If you said that your problem is world hunger, I'd question that you could solve such a problem. It is just too large and insurmountable to think that some lowly start-up is going to be able to solve it. I'd say it is "unsolvable" in any practical everyday meaning of being able to solve something (now, don't get upset and say that I'm claiming world hunger will never be solved; I'm just saying it's a big nut to crack and going to likely require more than a solo person starting up a company in their garage to get there).

For whatever the solvable problem might be, you need to then provide a viable solution. If you are saying that the solvable problem is that self-driving cars lack human driving capabilities due to not having common sense, presumably if your solution is to embody them with common sense, you need to have a viable means to get there.

One of the firms that pitched the common sense reasoning for AI self-driving cars could not describe how they are going to produce common sense. No one on the team knew much about the prior work on common sense reasoning. So, they seemed to have found a handy problem, one that might be solvable, but they had no clear path to a viable solution for it. This suggests that they might expend a tremendous amount of misguided effort and never land on a viable solution. In other words, yes, a solution might exist, but they didn't seem to know how to viably arrive at it.

Identified Problem and Claimed Solution Need to Match

It's also important that the identified problem and the claimed solution seem to match with each other. One of the startups that said they were going to create common sense reasoning, when I asked them what problem are they trying to solve, they said the problem to be solved is that it is arduous and unreliable to examine camera captured images for where pedestrians are.

Well, I agree that computerized visual processing techniques are not proficient yet at being able to find the images of pedestrians in captured pictures, but I questioned why common sense reasoning was needed to do so. It seemed to me that there are lots of other "non-common sense" reasoning approaches that can potentially get there. That being said, I certainly could see how common sense reasoning might help, but it's not really seemingly the primary aspect right now.

In this sense, it was as though the problem and the solution weren't necessarily lining up.

This misalignment can be even more pronounced. One startup said that the problem was that people aren't trusting of AI self-driving cars. The proposed solution was to improve the in-car entertainment capabilities by some electronic gadgetry they had put together. When I inquired as to why people would be more trusting of a self-driving car simply due to being able to say watch a live-stream movie while traveling in it, they mumbled an incomprehensible answer.

I tried to help them by suggesting that maybe the concept was that by being distracted within the self-driving car that maybe people would no longer be preoccupied with how the AI self-driving car is driving. Perhaps this would boost trust. Or, I said that maybe they were trying to provide a calming capability that would be a stress reducer. Maybe the stress reduction would somehow lead to people becoming more trusting of their self-driving car.

You can see that I was generously trying to help them dig themselves out of a hole. Not all judges will do so. Many love to help dig the hole deeper. It's not my style. If you've ever watched the Shark Tank television show, you probably know that there is one member of the judges that seems to relish putting an entrepreneur on the spot. I know it makes for good TV ratings. I'd prefer to find a means to constructively help budding entrepreneurs and don't believe that belittling them is the way to go. Of course, some of my colleagues insist that it is "tough love" that will harden the entrepreneur and also that "what doesn't kill them will make them stronger" kind of perspective.

I've mainly covered the first two factors in this discussion. Please take a close look at all 20 factors. Think about your start-up and what it is doing or going to be doing on each of the factors. If you want others to think you are serious about your start-up, you need to show some kind of consideration for each of the twenty factors. You might want to find a mentor that can help. Go to pitch competitions to watch and learn from others that are pitching, plus you might find a mentor there. If you make a pitch, try to see if you can chat with the judges afterward to get their direct feedback.

One of the points I often make at the pitch competitions is that many investors are looking as much for the jockey as the horse.

The horse is the nature of the start-up in terms of what it is and the focus of the start-up. The jockey is the entrepreneur that's founded and pushing forward on the start-up. By-and-large, start-ups are going to pivot and shift as they try to figure out the right focus. The question is whether the entrepreneur, as the jockey, whether they have the wherewithal to pivot and have the needed expertise or capabilities for the nature of the business. At times, ideas are a dime a dozen, but the entrepreneur that has the right stuff is often very hard to find. They are the diamond in the rough. Invest in them, and whatever the end-up doing will come out magnificently.

Hey, let me say that I wish you the best of luck for your start-up ambitions!

As a former university professor that taught courses on entrepreneurship, and also a seasoned serial entrepreneur (the buzzword is that a "serial" entrepreneur is one that has experience launching and running multiple start-ups over time), I can forewarn you that start-ups can be one of the greatest joys in your career, but can also shake you to the deepest depths of your soul.

You know the old line about how to get to Carnegie Hall? Answer, practice, practice, practice. How can you succeed as an entrepreneur? I always say it's persistence, persistence, persistence.

CHAPTER 3

CODE OBFUSCATION AND AI SELF-DRIVING CARS

CHAPTER 3

CODE OBFUSCATION AND
AI SELF-DRIVING CARS

Earlier in my career, I was hired to reverse engineer a million lines of code for a system that the original developer had long since disappeared. He had left behind no documentation. The firm had at least gotten him to provide a copy of the source code. Nobody at the firm knew anything about how the code itself worked. The firm was dependent upon the compiled code executing right and they simply hoped and prayed that they would not need to make any changes to the system.

Not a very good spot to be in.

I was told that the project was a hush-hush one and that I should not tell anyone else what I was doing. They would only let me see the source code while physically at their office, and otherwise I wasn't to make a copy of it or take it off the premises. They even gave me a private room to work in, rather than sitting in a cubicle or other area where fellow staffers were. I became my own miniature skunk works, of sorts.

There was a mixture of excitement and trepidation for me about this project. I had done other reverse engineering efforts before and knew how tough it could be to figure out someone else's code. Any morsels of "documentation" were always welcomed, even if the former developer(s) had only written things onto napkins or the back of recycled sheets of paper. Also, I usually had someone that kind of knew something about the structure of the code or at least had heard rumors by water cooler chats with the tech team. In this case, the only thing I had available were the end-users that used the system. I was able to converse with them and find out what the system was supposed to do, how they interacted with it, the outputs it produced, etc.

For a million lines of code, and with supposedly just one developer, he presumably was churning out a lot of lines of code for being just one person. I was told that he was a "coding genius" and that he was always able to "magically" make the system do whatever they needed. He was a great resource, they said. He was willing to make changes on the fly. He would come in during weekends to make changes. They felt like they had been given the "hacker from heaven" (with the word hacker in this case meaning a proficient programmer, and not the nowadays more common use as a criminal or cyber hacker).

I gently pointed out that if he was such a great developer, dare I say software engineer, how come he hadn't documented his work? How come no one else was ever able to lay eyes on his work? How come he was the only one that knew what it did? I pointed out that they had painted themselves into a corner. If this heavenly hacker got hit by a bus (and floated upstairs, if you know what I mean), what then?

Well, they sheepishly admitted that I must be some kind of mind reader because he had one day just gotten up and left the company. There were stories that his girlfriend had gotten kidnapped in some foreign country and that he had arranged for mercenaries to rescue her, and that he personally was going there to be part of the rescue team. My mouth gaped open at this story. Sure, I suppose it could be true. I kind of doubted it. Seemed bogus.

The whole thing smelled like the classic case of someone that was protective of their work, and also maybe wanted a bit of job security. It's pretty common that some developers will purposely aim to not document their code and make it as obscure as they can, in hopes of staving off losing their job. The idea is that if you are the only one that knows the secret sauce, the firm won't dare get rid of you. You will have them trapped. Many companies have gotten themselves into that same predicament. And, though it seems like an obvious ploy to you and me, these firms often are clueless about what is taking place and fall into the trap without any awareness. When the person suddenly departs, the firm wakes up "shockingly" to what they've allowed to happen.

Some developers that get themselves into this posture will also at times try to push their luck. They demand that the firm pay them more money. They demand that the firm let them have some special perks. They keep upping the ante figuring that they'll see how far they can push their leverage. This will at times trigger a firm to realize that things aren't so kosher. At that point, they often aren't sure of what to do. I've been hired as a "code mercenary" to parachute into such situations and try to help bail out the firm. As you might guess, the original developer, if still around, becomes nearly impossible to deal with and will refuse to lift a finger to help share or explain the secret sauce.

When I've discussed these situations with the programmer that had led things in that direction, they usually justified it. They would tell me that the firm at first paid them less than what a McDonald's hamburger slinger would get. They got no respect for having finely honed programming skills. If the firm was stupid enough to then allow things to get into a posture whereby the programmer now had the upper hand, it seems like fair play. The company was willing to "cheat" him, so why shouldn't he do likewise back to the company. The world's a tough place and we each need to make our own choices, is what I was usually told.

Besides, it often played out over months and sometimes years, and the firm could have at any time opted to do something to prevent the continuing and deepening dependency. One such programmer told me that he had "saved" the company a lot of money. The doing of documentation would have required more hours and more billable time. The act of showing the code to others and teaching them about how it worked, once again more billable time. Furthermore, just like the case that I began to describe herein, he had worked evenings and weekends, being at the beck and call of the firm. They had gotten a great deal and had no right to complain.

Anyway, I'll put to the side for the moment the ethics involved in all of this.

When I took a look at the code of the "man that went to save his girlfriend in a strange land," here's what I found: Ludwig Van Beethoven, Wolfgang Amadeus Mozart, Johann Sebastian Bach, Richard Wagner, Joseph Haydn, Johannes Brahms, Franz Schubert, Peter Ilyich Tchaikovsky, etc.

Huh?

Allow me to elaborate. The entire source code consisted of variables with names of famous musical composers, and likewise all of the structure and objects and subroutines were named after such composers or were based on titles of their songs. Instead of seeing something like LoopCounter = LoopCounter + 1, it would say Mozart = Mozart + 1. Imagine a financial banking application that instead of referring to Account Name, Account Balance, Account Type, it instead said Bach, Wagner, and Brahms, respectively.

So, when trying to figure out the code, you'd need to tease out of the code that whenever you see the use of "Bach" it really means the Account Name field. When you see the use of Wagner it really means the Account Balance. And so on.

I was kind of curious about this seeming fascination with musical composers. When I asked if the developer was known for perhaps having a passion for classical music, I was told that maybe so, but not that anyone noticed.

I'd guess that it wasn't so much his personal tastes in composers, and instead it was more likely his interest in code obfuscation.

You might not be aware that some programmers will purposely write their code in a manner to obfuscate it. They will do exactly what this developer had done. Instead of using naming that would be logically befitting the circumstance, they would make-up other names. The idea was that this would make it much harder for anyone else to figure out the code. This ties back to my earlier point about the potential desire to become the only person that can do the maintenance and upkeep on the code. By making things as obfuscated as you can, it causes anyone else to be either be baffled or have to climb up a steep learning curve to divine your secret sauce code.

If the person's hand was forced by the company insisting that they share the code with Joe or Samantha, the programmer could say, sure, I'll do so, and then hand them something that seems like utter mush. Here you go, have fun, the developer would say. If Joe and Samantha had not seen this kind of trickery before, they would likely roll their eyes and report back to management that it was going to be a long time to ferret out how the thing works.

I had the CEO of a software company that when this very thing happened, and when it was me that told him the programmer had made the code obfuscated, the CEO nearly blew his top. We'll sue him for every dime we ever paid him, the CEO exclaimed. We'll hang him out to dry and tell any future prospective employer that he's poison and don't ever hire him. And so on. Of course, trying to go after the programmer for this is going to be somewhat problematic. Did the code work? Yes. Did it do what the firm wanted? Yes. Did the firm ever say anything about the code having to be more transparently written? No.

Motivations for Code Obfuscation Vary

I realize that some of you have dealt with code that appears to be the product of obfuscation, and yet you might say that it wasn't done intentionally. Yes, I agree that sometimes the code obfuscation can occur by happenstance. A programmer that doesn't consider the ramifications of their coding practices might indeed write such code.

They maybe didn't intend to write something obfuscated, it just turned out that way. Suppose this programmer loved the classics and the composers, and when he started the coding he opted to use their names. That was well and good for say the first thousand lines of code.

He then kept building upon the initial base of code. Might as well continue the theme of using composer names. After a while, the whole darned thing is shaped in that way. It can happen, bit by bit. At each point in time, you think it doesn't make sense to redo what you've already done, and so you just keep going. It might be like constructing a building that you first laid down some wood beams for, and even if maybe you should be using steel instead because that building is actually ultimately going to be a skyscraper, you started with wood, you kept adding into it with wood, and so wood it is.

For those of you that have pride as a software engineer, these stories often make you ill to your stomach. It's those seat-of-the-pants programmers that give software development and software developers a bad name. Code obfuscation for a true software engineer is the antithesis of what they try to achieve. It's like seeing a bridge with rivets and struts made of paper and you know the whole thing was done in a jury rigged manner. That's not how you believe good and proper software is written.

I think we can anyway say this, code obfuscation can happen for a number of reasons, including possibly:

- Unintentionally and without awareness of it as a concern
- Unintentionally and by step at a time falling into it
- Intentionally and with some loathsome intent to obfuscate
- Intentionally but with an innocent or good meaning intent

So far, the intent to obfuscate has been suggested as something being done for job security or other personal reasons that have seemed somewhat untoward. There's another reason to want to obfuscate the code, namely for code security or privacy, and rightfully so.

Suppose you are worried that someone else might find the code. This someone is not supposed to have it. You want the code to remain relatively private and you are hopeful of securing it so that no one else can rip it off or otherwise see what's in it. This could be rightfully the case, since you've written the code and the Intellectual Property (IP) rights belong to you of it. Companies often invest millions of dollars into developing proprietary code and they obviously would like to prevent others from readily taking it or stealing it.

You might opt to encrypt the file that contains the source code. Thus, if someone gets the file, they need to find a means to decrypt it to see the contents. You can use some really strong form of encryption and hopefully the person wanting to inappropriately decrypt the file will have a hard time doing so and might be unable to do so or give up trying.

Using encryption is a pretty much an on-or-off kind of thing. In the encrypted state, no sense can be made of the contents, presumably. Suppose though that you realize that one way or another, someone has a chance of actually getting to the source code and being able to read what it says. Either they decrypt the file, or they happen to come along when it is otherwise in a decrypted state and grab up a copy of it, maybe they wander over to the programmer's desktop and put in a USB stick and quickly get a copy while it is in plaintext format.

So, another layer of protection would be to obfuscate the code. You render the code less understandable. This can be done by altering the semantics of the code. The example of the musical composer names showcases how you might do this obfuscation. The musical composer names are written in English and readily read. But, from a logical perspective, in the context of this code, it wouldn't have any meaning to someone else. The programmer(s) working on the code might have agreed that they all accept the idea that Bach means Account Name and Wagner means Account Balance.

Anyone else that somehow gets their hands on the code will be perplexed. What does Bach mean here? What does Wagner refer to? It puts those interlopers at a disadvantage. Rather than just picking up the code and immediately comprehending it, now they need to carefully study it and try to "reverse engineer" what it seems to be doing and how it is working.

This might require a laborious line-by-line inspection. It might take lots of time to figure out. Maybe it is so well obfuscated that there's no reasonable way to figure it out at all.

The code obfuscation can also act like a watermark. Suppose that someone else grabs your code, and they opt to reuse it in their own system. They go around telling everyone that it is their own code, written from scratch, and no one else's. Meanwhile, you come along and are able to take a look at their code. Imagine that you look at their code and observe that the code has musical composer names for all of the key objects in the code. Coincidence? Maybe, maybe not. It could be a means to try and argue that the code was ripped off from your code.

There are ways to programmatically make code obfuscated. Thus, you don't necessarily need to do so by hand. You can use a tool to do the code obfuscation. Likewise, there are tools to help you crack a code obfuscation. Thus, you don't necessarily need to do so entirely by hand.

In the case of the musical composer names, I might simply substitute the word "Bach" with the words "Account Name" and so on, which might make the code more comprehensible. The reality is that it isn't quite that easy, and there are lots of clever ways to make the code obfuscated that it is very hard to render it fully un-obfuscated. There is still often a lot of by-hand effort required.

In this sense, the use of code obfuscation can be by purposeful design. You are trying to achieve the so-called "security by obscurity" kind of trickery. If you can make something obscure, it tends to make it harder to figure out and break into. At my house, I might put a key outside in my backyard so that I can get in whenever I want, but of course a burglar can now do the same. I might put the key under the doormat, but that's pretty minimal obscurity. If I instead put the key inside a fake rock and I put it amongst a whole dirt area of rocks, the obfuscation is a lot stronger.

One thing about the source code obfuscation that needs to be kept in mind is that you don't want to alter the code such that it computationally does something different than what it otherwise was going to do. That's not usually considered in the realm of obfuscation. In other words, you can change the appearance of the code, you can possibly change around the code so that it doesn't seem as recognizable, but if you've now made it that the code can no longer calculate the person's banking balance, or if you've changed it such that the banking balance now gets calculated in a different way, you aren't doing just code obfuscation.

In quick recap, here's some aspects about code obfuscation:

- You are changing up the semantics and the look, but not the computational effect
- Code obfuscation can be done by-hand and/or by the use of tools
- Trying to reverse engineer the obfuscation can be done by-hand and/or by the use of tools
- There is weak obfuscation that doesn't do an extensive code obfuscation
- There is strong obfuscation that makes the code obfuscation deep and arcane to unwind
- Code obfuscation can serve an additional purpose of trying to act like a watermark

What does this have to do with AI self-driving cars?

At the Cybernetic AI Self-Driving Car Institute, we are developing AI software for self-driving cars. And, like many of the auto makers and tech firms, we consider the source code to be proprietary and worthy of protecting.

One means for the auto makers and tech firms to try and achieve some "security via obscurity" is to go ahead and apply code obfuscation to their precious and highly costly source code.

This will help too for circumstances where someone somehow gets a copy of the source code. It could be an insider that opts to leak it to another firm or sell it to a competitor. Or, it could be that an breach took place into the systems holding the source code and a determined attacker managed to grab it. At some later point in time, if the matter gets exposed and there is a legal dispute, it's possible that the code obfuscation aspects could come to play as a type of watermark of the original code.

If you are considering using code obfuscation for this kind of purpose, you'll obviously want to make sure that the rest of the team involved in the code development is on-board with the notion too. Some developers will like the idea, some will not. Some firms will say that when you check-out the code from a versioning system, they will have it automatically undo the code obfuscation, and only when it is resting in the code management system will it be in the code obfuscation form. Anyway, there are lots of issues to be considered before jumping into this.

Let's also remember that there are other ways that one can end-up with code obfuscation. For some of the auto makers and tech firms, and with some of the open source code that has been posted for AI self-driving cars, I've right away noticed a certain amount of code obfuscation that has crept into the code when I've gotten an opportunity to inspect it.

As mentioned earlier, it could be that the natural inclination of the programmers or AI developers involves writing code that has code obfuscation in it. This can be especially true for some of the AI developers that were working in university research labs and now they have taken a job at an auto maker or tech firm that is creating AI software for self-driving cars. In the academic environment, often any kind of code you want to sling is fine, no need to "pretty it up" since it usually is done as a one-off to do an experiment or provide some kind of proof about an algorithm.

Self-Driving Car Software Needs to be Well-Built

The software intended to run a self-driving car ought to be better made than that – lives are at stake.

In some cases, the AI developers are under such immense pressures to churn out code for a self-driving car, due to the auto maker or tech firm having unimaginable or unattainable deadlines, they inadvertently write code no matter whether it seems clear cut or not. As often has been said, there is no style in a knife fight. There can also be AI developers that aren't given guidance to write clearer code, or not given the time to do so, or not rewarded for doing so, and thus all of those reasons can come to play in code obfuscation too.

Per my framework about AI self-driving cars, these are the major tasks involved in the AI driving the car:

- Sensor data collection and interpretation
- Sensor fusion
- Virtual world model updating
- AI action plan formulation
- Car controls command issuance

There is a lot of code involved in each of those tasks. This is a real-time system that must be able to act and react quickly. The code needs to be tightly done so that it can run in optimal time. Meanwhile, the code needs to be understandable since the humans that wrote the code will need to find bugs in it, when they appear (which they will), and the humans need to update the code (such as when new sensors are added), and so on.

Some of the elements are based on "non-code" such as a machine learning model. Let's agree to carve that out of the code obfuscation topic for the moment, though there are certainly ways to craft a machine learning model that can be more transparent or less transparent. In any case, taking out those pre-canned portions, I assure you that there's a lot of code still leftover.

The auto makers and tech firms are in a mixed bag right now with some of them developing AI software for self-driving cars that is well written, robust, and ready for being maintained and updated. Others are rushing to write the code, or are unaware of the ramifications of writing obfuscated code, and might not realize the err of their ways until further along in the life cycle of advancing their self-driving cars. There are even some AI developers that are like the music man that wrote his code with musical composers in mind, for which it could be an unintentional act or an intentional act. In any case, it might be "good" for them right now, but likely later on will most likely turn out to be "bad" for them and others too.

Here's then the final rules for today's discussion on code obfuscation for AI self-driving cars:

- If it is happening and you don't realize it, please wake-up and decide what to overtly be doing

- If you are using it as a rightful technique for security by obscurity, please make sure you do so aptly

- If you are using it for nefarious purposes, just be aware that what goes around comes around

- If you aren't using it, decide explicitly whether to consider it or not, making a calculated decision about the value and ROI of using code obfuscation

For those of you reading this article, please be aware that in thirty seconds this text will self-obfuscate into English language obfuscation and the article will no longer appear to be about code obfuscation and instead will be about underwater basket weaving. The secrets of code obfuscation herein will no longer be visible. Voila!

CHAPTER 4
HYPERLANES AND
AI SELF-DRIVING CARS

CHAPTER 4

HYPERLANES AND
AI SELF-DRIVING CARS

I feel the need, the need for Maglev speed. The Maglev is considered the fastest commercial High-Speed Rail (HSR) line and whisks passengers at a breathtaking 267 miles per hour from the Pudong airport to the Longyang station in Shanghai, a distance just shy of 20 miles. Named the Maglev because it uses magnetic levitation, it has been a marvel since it first opened in 2004. There are other high-speed rail lines of a research nature that are faster than the Maglev but it still currently holds the top record for a commercial in-use line.

Let's call high-speed rail lines a more flavorful name, bullet trains. Of course, a bullet train cannot really go as fast as a bullet (which travels around 1,700 mph), though if you are standing on the sidelines when a bullet train goes past it might seem like it is going over a thousand miles per hour. We're not there yet. Those of us in the United States don't have many bullet train choices and the preponderance of bullet trains are found in Europe and Asia.

If you hold your breath, you might get a chance to someday ride a bullet train in California. That's actually a funny statement because anyone that lives in California knows that we've been pining away to have a bullet train for quite a long time. You'd need to have large pair of lungs to hold your breath for as long as we've contemplated having our very own California bullet train. In 2008, California residents voted in favor of Proposition 1A, a $9 billion bond to help kick-start a bullet train that would run from Los Angeles to San Francisco. Nearly seven years later, in 2015, there was an initial ground breaking ceremony that took place in Fresno, California.

Some liken the bullet train to waiting for Godot. It might or might not ever really happen. If it does happen, the guess is that it will be sometime in the 2030s before it is fully operational. The distance involved is quite a bit further than the Maglev that I mentioned earlier – the California bullet train will go a distance of about 438 miles. Recall that the Maglev went a scant 20 miles or so.

When you consider a bullet train and what it is, you need to be aware of the distance it goes and the intended average speed. The Maglev goes a very short distance of about 20 miles at a speed of 267 mph. For the California bullet train, the voters were told that it would likely have an operating speed of 220 mph. That's obviously slower than the Maglev, but pretty impressive when you consider that the distance covered is more than twenty times the distance involved. It's not easy to keep up a high speed over a lengthy distance.

You might find it curious that I've claimed that having a fast speed over a long distance is not an easy thing to achieve. If you've not ever seen a bullet train, you might not realize that to gain high speeds you typically need to have a really good track that is straight and level. The more that the track bends or curves, and the more that it rises or descends, these are all factors that impact the operating speed. Imagine trying to make a completely level track over a distance of over four hundred miles. Doing so through many populated areas. It's not readily feasible.

Furthermore, over a vast distance of several hundred miles, and in a place like California, you've got mountains you have to somehow deal with. There are three key mountain ranges that divide the northern part of California that has San Francisco from the southern part of California that contains Los Angeles. You can either route around mountains or opt to go directly through them. If you want the speed and you want to keep the distance low, going around a mountain is not usually a good choice. So, you need to tunnel into the mountain. That's costly and takes time to do.

There are bodies of water that you'll need to contend with. Viaducts. Farm land. And believe it or not, the bullet train in California is supposed to route through five of the ten most major cities in the entire state. Rights of way become an issue. Protecting the track from people is an issue. Protecting the track from animals is an issue. The headaches abound.

Not everyone wants the bullet train, and especially there are worrisome folks in some of the locations through which the bullet train will travel. Some locals in those impacted areas are worried about the noise of the bullet train. They worry about the vibrations it will cause. In some cases, they worry that travelers that might have driven their cars will now bypass the local areas and opt instead to take the bullet train. This could punish the local economy. Perhaps layoffs and businesses closing down, and families having to go elsewhere to find a means to make a living. This vaunted bullet train notion is not all rosy.

One ongoing question involves how the bullet train in California will impact the travelers going between the two locations in terms of mode of travel. In theory, the bullet train is intended to reduce the flights needed to get from San Francisco to Los Angeles. It is asserted that the planes produce more pollutants than would the bullet train. It is asserted that the cost per passenger per mile will be lessened by the bullet train over travel by flight.

You need to know that a flight from LAX to San Francisco is usually about an hour and a half in duration, which is important when considering the bullet train alternative. Business travelers that are not especially price sensitive are going to focus not so much on the lower cost presumably of the bullet train travel, but how long it takes them to make the distance. To-date, the California bullet train authority has said that it will be a time of 2 hours and 40 minutes. Thus, it would apparently take about an hour longer via the bullet train than flying.

Many object to the comparison of the times because of other factors involved. When you go to an airport such as LAX, you are supposed to get there two hours before your flight. You need to check your bags. You need to go through security. Etc. The bullet train advocates point out that when you get onto the bullet train, you don't need to have those same delays and inconveniences. They would claim that if you add the real amount of time involved to the flights, you'd say a flight takes much longer overall than the forecasted bullet train travel time.

Bullet train advocates say that besides reducing the number of flights, the advent of the bullet train will pull people out of their polluting gas-guzzling cars too. They claim that besides the environmental improvement, the cost per passenger per mile is going to be much better for the bullet train than going via conventional car. It is claimed that perhaps 1.2 persons per car tend to drive the Los Angeles to San Francisco corridor and so it is highly inefficient, including from an energy consumption perspective.

The maximum speed limit for cars in California is legally stated as 65 mph, though in some areas it is allowed for drivers to go 70 mph. If you take the 438 miles distance of the proposed bullet train, and divide it by 70 mph, the projected time by driving a car would be 6 hours. You could argue that you are unlikely to be able to go 70 mph that entire distance. Perhaps due to traffic. Perhaps due to debris on the roadway. Perhaps due to foul weather. And so on.

Let's just assume for the moment that you could go 70 mph the whole way. One advantage of taking your car is that you are able to go from door to door. In other words, with a plane, you need to get to an airport before your start your journey, and so in theory you should count that local time, along with the waiting time at the airport. You could make the same case about the bullet train, namely that even if the waiting time is relatively low, it still isn't taking you from door to door.

Furthermore, let's be realistic and agree that Californians do not all abide by the stated speed limit. I assure you that when I've driven the LA/SF distance, the cars are pretty much all doing 80 mph, maybe 85 mph. It is not uncommon to find some cars that decide they are able to see how fast they can go, and at times they zip past me at a brazen 100 mph or more. There are vocal Californians that say we should not be limited by federal guidelines on our open highways and that we ought to have much higher speed limits for them. Some say it should even be like the German Autobahn that in some stretches does not have a posted maximum speed limit at all.

You might be aware that the United States national speed limit guidelines were developed partially due to the concerns about gas consumption, based on charts that showed that higher speeds tended to guzzle gas more so. This was considered a primary factor (occurring during the oil crisis), while other factors included that at high speeds there was the danger that an accident could be worsened, and that an accident would trigger a domino effect of other cascading accidents. If you are driving at a very high speed and an accident happens up ahead of you, your reaction time is reduced and your ability to maneuver or stop your rocketing car is reduced.

Suppose you could somehow maintain an operating speed of 85 mph on the 438 miles distance. This would mean that you'd get to San Francisco from LA in about 5 hours. Suppose you were willing to edge your car up to 100 mph? The distance could be covered in 4 ½ hours. Plus, that's with door to door convenience.

The bullet train advocates would point out that you'd be better off to drive to your local bullet train station in Los Angeles or in San Francisco and take the 2 hours and 40 minute bullet train instead. In the bullet train, you have room to move around. You don't need to worry about other cars that might cause a wreck, as you would if you were driving the distance. And, perhaps most significantly, you can leave the driving to the bullet train. You don't need to watch the road and be panicked about whatever the road ahead has, instead, you can leisurely look out the window of the bullet train and enjoy the scenery.

What does this have to do with AI self-driving cars?

At the Cybernetic AI Self-Driving Car Institute, we are developing AI software for self-driving cars. One aspect of the future for self-driving cars will be their ability to operate in a high-speed long-distance mode.

Let's consider what you could do in terms of using an AI self-driving car to make the ride that the California bullet train is proposing to do.

First, assuming that the AI self-driving car is a true Level 5 self-driving car, you don't need to worry about the driving aspects. A Level 5 self-driving car is one that can be driven by the AI and needs no human driver to intervene. Indeed, the Level 5 self-driving car won't likely have pedals and nor a steering wheel provided. Presumably, the AI does all the driving. Plus, it is supposed to drive as well as a human could, perhaps even better in some circumstances.

The point being that with a true AI self-driving car, you would not need to be driving the LA/SF and could enjoy the ride as a passenger, similar to what you would do on the bullet train or on an airplane. In that sense, the AI self-driving car is certainly superior to a conventional car that requires a human driver and so the comparison of the bullet train to a conventional car differs with an AI self-driving car.

On a related aspect, it is anticipated that likely most AI self-driving cars will be Electrical Vehicles (EVs). This does not need to be the case, but it's highly likely. The reason I mention this aspect is that the bullet train advocates emphasize that gas guzzling cars are polluters. An AI self-driving car that is based on an EV platform will take away that argument and thus remove the pollution differences consideration.

Someone that is reading this and perhaps is a bullet train advocate will probably say that Lance, you just tried to pull a fast one about those EVs. Most EVs today average maybe 100 to 150 miles distance before a recharge is needed. Thus, trying to drive the 438 miles of LA/SF would require about 4 stops to do a series of needed recharges. Even a fast recharger will still add a lot of time to the total time of having the AI self-driving car get you the distance involved after all of those needed stops.

I grant you that today's EVs have a distance capability that is more suited to short-distance hops, such as the average daily commute to work and home. But, please note that the Chevy Bolt can get about 238 miles on a single charge. The Tesla Model S can get about 337 miles. Those seem like outliers now, but the EV makers all realize that without being able to cover larger distances, the masses aren't going to be willing to buy EVs. There is a tremendous effort going on to increase battery capacities and I think it's reasonable to expect that we'll relatively soon be able to go the 438 miles on a single charge.

Remember that the bullet train is not expected to be in use until the 2030s. Give the EV makers a few years from now and we'll likely see vast improvements in distance coverage, long before the 2030s.

A true AI self-driving car then could be a non-polluter, it would drive the car for you, and potentially go the distance in one stretch. In terms of being able to freely move around, which you can do in a bullet train, admittedly in an AI self-driving car you won't quite have the same physical freedoms, but it is anticipated that the interior of AI self-driving cars will be completed redesigned from today's conventional cars. It is envisioned that you'll likely have swivel chairs, allowing you to face others in the self-driving car, and possibly a bed-like capability so that you can sleep while in the AI self-driving car.

The biggest catch might be the speed aspects. Do we want these true AI self-driving cars to be going at high speeds? What is the boundary we are comfortable with? Will maintaining a speed of 85 mph be acceptable, which seems like it would since its pretty much the norm now anyway. Some would say they see nothing wrong with aiming at a speed of 100 mph. Others would push the envelope and argue that 125 mph would be acceptable.

At a speed of 125 mph, the 438 mile distance of SF/LA would take about 3 ½ hours. That's getting pretty darned close to the supposed 2 hours and 40 minutes for the bullet train. As an aside, there are many that argue with the alleged 2 hours and 40 minutes by the bullet train authority, and point out that this is only based on computer based simulations of what might be possible. And, it is suggested that those simulations have questionable assumptions about what the bullet train will really do when encountering the various aspects of how the bullet train is really going to be constructed.

You might also find of interest the price tag for the California bullet train. The price has been going up each passing year, apparently due to re-estimating and also due to deeper explorations about what the construction will consist of. The price tag had been around $33 billion. Now, its ballooned to about $77 billion. Some say there is no end in sight.

For AI self-driving cars, you might say that there is no construction cost per se, since these AI self-driving cars are going to be able to traverse the distance without any kind of special capability. In essence, an everyday true AI self-driving car can make the drive. The road does not need any special construction or alteration. Humans can drive the distance today. So, the AI self-driving cars should be able to do so too.

We could though try to level the playing field by looking at the chances of accidents and the safety factor. Bullet trains have been remarkably safe. Very few accidents. Would the true AI self-driving cars be able to match that kind of safety record?

The stretch of highway from LA to SF that is usually undertaken for making the fastest drive between those south and north locations is Interstate 5. Interstate 5 is a north-south highway that seems to be kept in relatively good shape and is highly passable. There are also ongoing efforts by the CalTrans authority to keep the highway clean of debris, which admittedly can be challenging since people seem to transport their belongings often in open bed trucks and I've seen chairs, mattresses, and other items dropped onto the 5 during my various travels on that path. Another frequent inhabitant is the mauled rubber from blown out tires, and an occasional carcass of roadkill.

Overall, in my experience, it's been rare that my drive on the I-5 has been delayed due to debris. The most common delay is due to traffic. There are two lanes in each direction, and sometimes the traffic gets so voluminous it seems to swamp the lanes. Plus, you get a driver doing 50 mph in one lane that forces the faster traffic over into the fast lane, but then the slow driver also opts to get into the fast lane. There's also a lot of goods carrying trucks that make this haul and they tend to abide by the 55 mph speed limit.

All in all, it would seem that the I-5 might have some troubles trying to ensure that true AI self-driving cars could go along at an operating speed of say 100 mph or higher, not due to the road itself and not due to debris, but more so to the traffic control.

That being said, one of the potential aspects about AI self-driving cars involves their ability to communicate with each other using V2V (vehicle to vehicle communications), and possibly V2I (vehicle to infrastructure communications). As such, the AI self-driving cars could communicate electronically to coordinate their movement on the I-5. This would presumably allow for speedy lane changes and avoid lane blockages. There has been work done on AI self-driving cars working together in "swarms" and the use of this approach on the LA/SF stretch would make sense.

In terms of the chances of an AI self-driving car getting involved in a domino like car accident, this is something that still could happen, even with true AI self-driving cars and there using V2V and V2I. Some AI self-driving car pundits seem to believe in the "zero fatalities" mantra about AI self-driving cars. I don't. If an AI self-driving car is traveling at 100 mph and a deer darts onto the highway, there's no getting around the physics of getting the car to stop in time and avoid hitting the deer (assuming that it was unable to be detected prior). That could happen in even an all AI self-driving cars on the roadways scenario.

One important additional consideration is the mixture of human drivers and AI self-driving cars on the roadways. As I've mentioned many times, we are not going to anytime soon have only AI self-driving cars on our roads.

Many of the self-driving car pundits talk about a nirvana world in which there are only AI self-driving cars. This would remove the human driver and allow the AI to fully coordinate the driving aspects.

But, it is important to realize that today there are about 200+ million conventional cars in the United States alone. Those conventional cars are not going to magically be turned into AI self-driving cars overnight. For many years, there are going to be a mixture of human driven cars and AI self-driving cars.

As such, we are then in a bit of a predicament or conundrum because it seems as though true AI self-driving cars could potentially be a viable alternative to or complimentary to a bullet train, but not if we can't do something about the traffic aspects. The roadway seems plausible to be used, and our main concern in this case involves the car traffic rather than the roadway itself.

You could opt to dictate that only true AI self-driving cars could go on the I-5. This is likely to create a widespread public backlash. It would be perceived that those elitist owned AI self-driving cars have taken over a key public roadway and a vital connector between northern and southern California. This might be hard to convince the public at large to accept.

Another approach would be to "transform" the I-5 into a so-called hyperlane. This might consist of expanding the number of lanes and dedicating some of the lanes for exclusive use by the true AI self-driving cars. The remaining lanes could be used by conventional car traffic. This dual lane division would separate the two, allowing the speedy and V2V communicating AI self-driving cars to use their own space for trying to maintain top operating speeds. Conventional car drivers would have less to complain about since they presumably would still be able to drive on the I-5.

The lane expansion might be to widen the existing road, as mentioned above. Or, some might argue to go over the top of the existing lanes and provide an aerial or raised alternative. Going underground beneath the existing road would seem prohibitive. In whatever way it might be undertaken, there's certainly a hefty cost to this infrastructure change. Would we better off spending the $77 billion on the bullet train or some (or all of it) on transforming the I-5 to become a hyperlane?

Should we consider having both the bullet train and the hyperlane?

This would require a belief that the traffic will be so voluminous that both approaches are needed.

Some would argue that neither approach is warranted because we'll "soon" hopefully have flying cars or drones that can carry people. If we can transport people in the air, doing so via individual or small group transport, would that be "better" than conventional airplanes, and/or better than a bullet train or ground-based self-driving cars? Lots of potential options, no clear cut answers.

Overall, will the advent of AI self-driving cars spell the death knell for bullet trains? If we have zillions of true AI self-driving cars on our roadways, and if they are the energizer of the ridesharing economy, it could be that the notion of and adoption of bullet trains is no longer prudent. It's hard to say right now whether and when we'll have widespread true AI self-driving cars. In the meantime, the bullet train still holds promise, but only in circumstances that showcase how the bullet train is justifiable, given its myriad of infrastructure and societal requirements. I'd advise taking a ride on a bullet train as soon as you can, in case they eventually become extinct.

CHAPTER 5

PASSENGER PANIC INSIDE AN AI SELF-DRIVING CAR

CHAPTER 5

PASSENGER PANIC INSIDE
AN AI SELF-DRIVING CARS

Don't panic. Wait, change that, go ahead and panic. Are you panicked yet?

Sometimes people momentarily lose their minds and opt to panic. This primal urge can be handy as it invokes the classic fight-or-flight instinctive reaction to a situation. If you suddenly see a bear up ahead while in the woods, it could be that rather than carefully trying to plot out all of the myriad of options about what to do, entering instead into a panic mode might get your feet moving and you'll have run far from the bear before it has had a chance to do anything to you. On the other hand, it could be that your effort to run away is not wise and the bear easily catches up with you, allowing the bear to win and perhaps an untoward result for you.

Not many of us will likely get into a circumstance of confronting a bear, and so let's consider something that might be higher odds of happening to any of us. Suppose you are in an airplane and the plane is on the ground and engaged in fire. Presumably, with or without panic, you'd realize that you should get out of the burning airplane.

How can you get out of the burning airplane? I'm sure you've all sat through the flight attendants telling you to figure out beforehand the nearest exit to your seat. I'd bet that most people don't look to see where that exit is, and instead just kind of assume that when there's an emergency they'll figure out where the exit is. Or, they'll simply follow everyone else, under the assumption that everyone else knows where the exit is and that they are heading toward it.

Interestingly, recent studies seem to show that when people are in a burning airplane and you would assume they would be heading toward the exit as fast as they could, they actually often try to grab their belongings from the overhead bin first. This creates a significant delay. This creates heightened risk of getting caught inside the burning airplane. This creates the strong possibility of dying on-board the plane. Yet, people do this anyway, in spite of the seemingly obvious aspect that you should just get off the plane.

There was a flight out of Cancun that included 169 passengers and 6 crew members, and while on the ground the plane started to get engulfed with flames. Some of the passengers opted to try and retrieve their bags before getting out of the plane. The evacuation time took over three minutes. Tests done with people getting out of the same sized plane have indicated that it should take about ninety seconds. The difference in the doubling of the time in actual practice could have led to deaths (fortunately, no deaths occurred in this Cancun instance).

A more dramatic example would be the Air France A340 in Canada that ran off the runway and the plane split into two pieces, including erupting into flames. Reports afterward indicated that about half of the passengers first retrieved their bags before getting off the plane. Remarkably, this occurred while the flight attendants were yelling to get out of the plane and not first grab your bags. I guess keeping your toothbrush safe and your other personal items in the bag that's jammed into the overhead bin is worth possibly losing your life over.

Let's also clarify that this act of grabbing your bag is more than just one that can harm you. It's one thing if you do something ill-advised and it is only you that can get hurt from it, but in the case of an airplane, the act of grabbing your bag is undoubtedly going to create a delay for other humans trying to get past you to exit from that plane. So, it's not just a personal choice with personal consequences, it's a choice that involves deciding whether other people should also suffer a worse fate because of your decision.

That's an important added twist to this discussion about panic. When a person panics while in a crowd, it can have spreading consequences like a kind of virus. One person grabs their bag, it slows down everyone else. The slowing down of others might cause them to panic more so. Their getting into a deeper panic might cause them to do something untoward, and the cycle keeps repeating with others all doing things to indirectly or directly harm others.

Indeed, it is believed that often times the grabbing of the bag in the burning airplane is done partially because others are doing a copycat. They see one person that does it, and they opt to do the same. This could be a monkey-see, monkey-do kind of reaction. Or, it could be a follow-the-leader reaction, namely they assume that the other person knows something they don't know, such as maybe it is prudent to grab your bag, and so they follow that leader. Or, it could be a competitive juices kind of thing, wherein you think if that person gets to keep their bag intact, you should be able to do so too.

Or, it could also be that since the other person has now created a delay by getting their bag, others might think they might as well also create a delay, but in their minds they figure they are just using the delay time that the other person has created. In other words, I see a person grab for their bag, and I calculate that the person has now created a delay of some kind. During that momentary period of delay, I'll grab my bag too. Thus, I've not expanded the delay time, and instead merely efficiently used the otherwise already created delay time, and put it to good use that otherwise the time would have been me just watching the other person grab their bag.

How's that for some impressive logic?

It turns out there are other adverse consequences beyond just the time delay of getting a bag. People that are carrying a bag are typically going to take longer to get down the aisles and to the exit. Thus, they not only delayed others by grabbing their bag, the act of carrying the bag adds more delay too.

Furthermore, there are documented instances whereby the person carrying their bag came to the exit, saw that the chute that was inflated, and decided to toss their bag onto the chute, doing so before they jumped into the chute to slide down it. In some cases, the tossed bag actually punctured the chute. In other cases, the tossed bag hit other people on the chute, or blocked the chute and made it harder for others to slide down the chute. Similarly, the person that opts to keep their bag in their own clutches is likely to be a heavier and more awkward of a slider down the chute, often taking longer or hitting others on the chute.

In terms of the nature of panic, it is tempting to think that since on an airplane you already are vaguely aware that something can go amiss, and since the flight attendants at the start of the flight warn you about things that can go amiss, presumably there would not be much panic during an actual incident. People were forewarned that something can happen. If you are in the woods, maybe you didn't anticipate that a bear might appear in front of you. Maybe no one warned you beforehand that these particular woods have bears. On a plane, you would certainly be aware that the plane can go on fire and that you might need to exit quickly.

I realize that you might quibble with me about the "panic" aspects of the people on the plane that grabbed their bags. You might try to argue that they weren't panicked and instead mentally carefully weighed the risks of deciding whether to get their bags or not. In a very rational way, they decided that they had time to get their bags and that it was worthwhile to do so. If you watch videos of some of these incidents, I would suggest you see more panic-like reaction than what seems to be a chess match kind of consideration of what to do.

Overall, I'll concede that there are ranges of panic. You've got your everyday typical panic. You've got the panic that is severe and the person is really crazed and out of their head. You've got the person that seems to be continually in a semi-panic mode, no matter what the situation. And so on.

We'll use these classifications for now:

- No panic

- Mild panic

- Panic (everyday style)

- Severe panic

These forms of panic can be one-time, they can be intermittent, they can be persistent. Therefore, the frequency can be an added element to consider:

- One-time panic (of any of the aforementioned kinds)

- Intermittent panic

- Persistent panic

We can also add another factor, which some would debate fervently about, namely deliberate panic versus happenstance panic.

Most of the time, for most people, when they get into a panic mode, it is happenstance panic. It happens, and they have no or little control over it. It is like a wave of the ocean water that rises, reaches a crescendo, and then dissipates. There are some though that claim they are able to consciously use panic to their advantage. They wield it like a tool. As such, if the circumstance warrants, they force themselves to deliberately go into a panic mode. It is hoped or assumed that doing so might give them herculean strength or otherwise get their adrenalin going. This is somewhat debated about whether you can truly harness panic and use it like a domesticated horse.

In any case, here's these factors:

- Happenstance panic (most of the time)

- Deliberate directed panic (rare)

Let's consider how panic can come to play when driving a car.

If you watch a teenage novice driver, you are likely to see moments of panic. When they are first learning to drive, they are often quite fearful about the driving task and the dangers involved in driving a car (rightfully so!). As long as the driving task is coming along smoothly, they are able to generally keep their wits about them. This is why it is usually safest to start by having them drive in an empty parking lot. There's nothing to be distracted by, there are less things that can get hit, etc.

Suppose a teenage novice driver is driving in a neighborhood and a dog darts out from behind some bushes. For more seasoned drivers, this is something that is likely predictable and that you've seen before. You might apply the brakes or take other evasive actions, and do so without much panic ensuing. In contrast, the novice driver might begin to feel their blood pumping through their body, their heart seems to pound incessantly, their hands grip the steering wheel with a death like grasp, their body tenses up, they lean forward trying to see every inch of the road, and so on.

Should I hit the brakes, they are thinking. Should I try to accelerate past the dog? Should I honk the horn? Should I swerve? What to do? Their mind can become muddled and overwhelmed. They might pick any of those driving options and do so out of pure panic and not due to having decided which approach was the most prudent in the situation. They probably wouldn't have the presence of mind to look in their rear view mirror to see what is behind them, which would be handy to know, since if they do hit their brakes it could cause the car behind them to ram into their car.

Besides taking some kind of driving related action, the novice driver might do other things such as yell at the dog, which might not be sensible if the windows of the car are rolled up anyway and the dog couldn't hear you. Or, maybe you might flail your arms, taking them off the steering wheel, as though you are trying to motion at the dog to inform it to take action like getting out of the road. These motions might have little value and not be sensible in the circumstance, but panic often leads to people doing seemingly senseless things (like grabbing their bag when exiting a burning airplane!).

What does this have to do with AI self-driving cars?

At the Cybernetic AI Self-Driving Car Institute, we are developing AI software for self-driving cars. One important aspect involves considering what humans might do while inside an AI self-driving car and how to cope with their potential panic.

For the case of the dog that darts out into the street, let's change the scenario and assume that you are in an AI self-driving car. The AI is driving the car. You are not driving the car. Indeed, let's go with the notion that this is a Level 5 self-driving car, which is considered the level at which the AI is the sole driver of the car. There isn't any provision let's say for you, as a human, to be able to drive the car. There's no pedals, there isn't a steering wheel. The driving is entirely up to the AI system.

You are an occupant in the car. Maybe you were reading the newspaper and enjoying having the AI drive you around the neighborhood. Out of the corner of your eye, you see that a dog has suddenly darted into the street. What do you do?

For those of us that have grown-up in an era of cars that allow humans to drive the car, I'd bet that you'd be very tempted to want to suddenly take control of the car. You might instinctively reach for where the steering wheel used to be placed, or you might use your leg and jam downward instinctively as though you are slamming on the brakes. But, in this case, none of that is going to do any good. You are not driving the car.

As an aside, if we do ever become a society where only the AI is the driver, and you have people that have never driven a car themselves, I would guess that they won't react as you do, in that they aren't going to be tempted to "drive" the car, since they have always accepted the notion that it's up to the AI to do so. Eerie, kind of.

Anyway, back to that poor dog that's run into the street and is facing potential injury or death at the hands of the AI. You can see that the dog is possibly going to get hit. You likely are hoping or assume that the AI is going to detect the dog being there, and will take some kind of evasive maneuver. But, in those few seconds between your realization of the situation and before the AI has overtly reacted, you aren't sure what the AI is going to do. You don't even yet know if the AI realizes that the dog is there.

I suppose if you were someone that doesn't care about dogs or animals, you might just slump back into your seat in the car and shrug off the situation. You might think that if the car hits the dog, so be it. If the car misses the dog, so be it. Leave this up to the AI. You don't have a dog in this fight (a great pun!).

Perhaps you have blind faith in the AI and so you again slump back in your seat. You are calm because you know that the AI will make "the right decision" which might be to avoid the dog, or might be to hit the dog since maybe it's the lesser choice of two evils (perhaps if the AI were to swerve the car, it might injure or kill you, and so it chooses instead to hit the dog).

I'm betting that the odds are high that you'll actually be very concerned about the welfare of the dog, and also be concerned too about what the AI is going to do as a driving aspect. If the AI makes a wild maneuver, maybe it goes off the road and runs into a tree, and you get injured. Perhaps the AI doesn't recognize that there's a dog ahead and isn't going to do anything other than straight out hit the dog. This could harm or kill the dog, and likely damage the car, and you might get hurt too.

Well, in this situation, you might panic.

You could potentially wave frantically in hopes that the dog will see you, but this is low odds because the car has tinted windows and the windows are all rolled-up. You might wave your arms anyway, similar to what the novice example earlier suggested might be done. You might yell or scream. You might start crying, doing so because you believe the dog is about to get harmed and your body is reacting in the moment. Your heart starts pounding, you are frantic because you can see what is about to happen but have little or no control to avert the situation.

Here's a question for you to ponder – what should the AI do?

Now, I'm not referring to whether the AI should hit the dog or avoid the dog, I'm instead asking what the AI should do about you, the human occupant of the self-driving car.

Few of the auto makers and tech firms are considering that question right now.

They are so focused on getting an AI self-driving car to do the everyday driving task that they consider the aspects of the human occupants to be an "edge" problem. An edge problem is one that is considered not at the core of a problem. It's something that you figure you'll get to when you get to it. It's not considered primary. It's considered secondary to whatever else is primary.

The AI in our scenario is presumably focusing on the dog and what to do about the driving. That's suitable and sensible. Should it though also consider the humans inside the self-driving car? Should it be observing the humans to see how they are doing? Should it be listening for the humans to possibly say something that maybe the AI needs to know?

Suppose you were driving a car and you had a passenger in the car with you. A dog runs out into the street. The passenger in your car says to you, hey, watch out, there's a dog there. Maybe you, as the driver, were looking to the side of the road and had not noticed the dog. Thank goodness that the passenger noticed the dog and alerted you about it. You now see the dog and take evasive action. Dog saved. Humans saved.

If the AI of the self-driving car is only paying attention to the outside world, it might miss something that a passenger inside the AI self-driving car might have noticed that it didn't notice. Could be that the passenger provides valuable and timely information, similar to my example about the dog running into the street.

As a human driver, you already know that sometimes a passenger in your car might panic. They might see that dog, your passenger yells and screams about the dog, flails their arms, and you meanwhile are trying to keep a cool head. Yes, you see the dog. Yes, you are going to take appropriate driving action. The passenger doesn't necessarily know this. They are just in a panic mode. They are yelling and screaming, and maybe things even worse they try to reach over and grab the wheel from you. That could be quite dangerous.

Would we want the AI to be like that calm driver that also is allowing the passenger(s) in the self-driving car to provide input, which might or might not be useful, which might or might not be timely, or do we want the AI to completely ignore the human occupants?

It is our belief that the AI should be observing the human occupants in a mode that involves gaining their input, but that it also needs to be tempered by the situation and cannot just obediently potentially do whatever the human might utter. There is already going to be a need to have interaction between the AI and the human occupants, which will arise naturally in the course of being in the self-driving car and traveling, such as the human wanting to stop someplace to get food or go to the bathroom, or the human to ask the AI to slow down so the person can see the scenery, etc.

We also believe that it will be important for the AI to at times explain what it is doing and why. If the AI had told the human occupants that there was a dog in the road and that the AI was going to do a swerve to avoid it, the human occupants would be at least reassured that the AI realized the dog was there and that the AI was going to take action. This interaction with the human occupants can be tricky, such as in the case of the dog in the road there might not be sufficient time to forewarn the human occupants and the tight time frame needed to react might preclude providing an explanation.

Just like you aren't supposed to yell "Fire!" in a crowded theatre (unless there is a fire, presumably), the AI cannot blindly do whatever the human might say. Suppose the human tells the AI to come to an immediate halt and should slam on the brakes, and yet let's say the self-driving car is going 80 miles per hour on a crowded freeway and there is a semi-truck right on the heels of the self-driving car? Does hitting the brakes in that scenario make sense? Likely not.

So, the AI needs to realize that the input to the driving task by a human occupant will need to be filtered and gauged as based on the situation. Furthermore, if the human seems to be panicked, this could be a further indicator of being cautious about whatever the human has to say. If you were a human driver and the passenger next to you seemed utterly panicked, I dare say you would likely consider their advice to be dubious and not give it as much weight in comparison to if it seemed to be carefully reasoned.

Let's pursue further the overall notion of a human occupant and the nature of panic.

Suppose the AI is driving the Level 5 self-driving car and it's a nice quiet and easy going drive. The human occupant is reading the newspaper. They read a story about how the stock market is dropping. The person realizes their life savings is being drained away. They go into a panic mode. They start yelling for no apparent reason. They seem out of their head.

Most AI developers for self-driving cars would say that this is something that has nothing to do with the driving task, therefore, the AI has nothing to do with the situation. The AI should just keep driving the car. It makes no difference that the human is going nuts. If the matter doesn't pertain to hitting a dog up ahead in the roadway, or some other matter directly linked to the driving, it has no relevance to the AI.

But, if a human was driving the car, and they had a passenger that started uncontrollably weeping or otherwise went into a panic mode, what would the human driver do? I'd bet that even if you were in an Uber or Lyft, and maybe even if in a taxi, the human driver would say something to you. Are you OK? What's wrong? Besides asking those kind of questions, it might be handy to ask too because suppose that their panic has to do with the driving of the car? You don't know for sure that it does not. It might be handy to ascertain whether there is a connection between their apparent panic and the driving task.

Whatever underlies the panic, it could be that the panic somehow becomes pertinent to the driving task. Suppose the human occupant needs to be taken to the hospital because they believe they are having a heart attack (maybe it's just a panic attack that feels like a heart attack)? Or, maybe they are genuinely injured and need medical care. Or, suppose the human occupant desperately needs to meet with a friend and the friend lives up ahead a mile or two? In essence, the panic of the human occupant could lead to a needed change related to the driving task, whether it be to alter where the self-driving car is going, or even how the self-driving car is being driven (such as slow down, speed-up).

It is anticipated that most AI self-driving cars will have cameras pointed not only outward to detect the surroundings of the car, but also inward too. These inward facing cameras will be handy for when you might have your children in the self-driving car, doing so without adult supervision, and you would want to see how they are doing. Or, if you are using the AI self-driving car as a ridesharing service, you'd likely want to see how people are behaving inside the car and whether they are wrecking it. All in all, there is more than likely going to be inward facing cameras.

With the use of these inward facing cameras, the AI has the possibility of being able to detect that someone is having a panic moment. Besides the audio detection by the person's words or noises, the camera could be used in a facial recognition type of mode. Today's facial recognition can generally ascertain if someone seems happy or sad. It won't be long before the facial recognition will be coupled with body recognition, being able to then more comprehensively detect someone's mood and demeanor.

The AI could try to aid a person that's in a panic mode.

For example, the AI system might seek to calm the person and reassure them. The AI system could offer to connect with a loved one or maybe even 911. Some believe that we'll eventually have AI systems that act in a mental therapist manner, which would be easy then to include into the AI add-ons for the AI self-driving car. Of course, this calming effort should not detract from the AI that is intended to be operating the self-driving car, and thus any use of processors or system memory for the calming effort would need to be undertaken judiciously. Other considerations include should the AI open the windows to let in fresh air, or would it be better to keep the windows closed (maybe the panicked human might try to jump out the window!). Should the AI come to stop to let the human out, or is it safer for the human to stay inside the car. These are tough choices to be made.

Help, I've fallen down and I can't get up. That's the famous refrain from a commercial that gained great popularity. Suppose instead we use "I'm panicking inside this AI self-driving car and I don't know what do" and the question arises as to what the AI of the self-driving car will do.

We assert that the AI needs to be aware of the human occupants and be attentive in case they panic. The panic might be directly related to some aspect of the AI driving task. Or, it might not be related, but the AI might end-up having to alter the driving task due to the panic mode of the human. Furthermore, the AI could potentially try to aid the human in a manner that a fellow human passenger might or that perhaps even a human therapist might.

The odds are that people are going to become panicked when in an AI self-driving car to the degree that they are unsure or feel uneasy about the AI driving the car. There will be many human occupants that will become "back seat drivers" in that they are desirous of giving advice to the self-driving car, and also reacting as to the driving by the AI. Some AI developers have even suggested that the human occupants should not be allowed to look out the windows of the self-driving car, since all that it will do is get those pesky humans into a panic mode whenever the AI needs to make a tricky maneuver.

Some believe that the AI does not have any obligation to placate or aid the human occupants. In this view, the AI drives the car. Period. It's like a chauffeur that will only listen to you about whether to drive to home or to the store, and nothing else.

Maybe the initial versions of the AI would be that simplistic, but it would seem unwise to stop there. The AI needs to be fully able to contend with all aspects of the driving task, which means not just the pure mechanics of driving down a street and making turns. It means instead to be the captain of the ship, so to speak, and be able to aid the passengers, even when they go into a panic. Of course, we also need to make sure that the AI doesn't itself go into a panic mode. But, that's a story for another day.

CHAPTER 6

TECH
STOCKHOLM SYNDROME
AND
SELF-DRIVING CARS

CHAPTER 6

TECH STOCKHOLM SYNDROME
AND SELF-DRIVING CARS

You might be vaguely aware of the Stockholm Syndrome. From time-to-time, the news media will refer to a situation as somehow invoking the famous case of what happened in the 1970's in Stockholm, Sweden. In that case, bank robbers in Stockholm took several hostages and holed-up in the bank vault for six days, refusing to come out and refusing to give up the hostages. Once the siege ended, the hostages surprisingly later on refused to testify against the kidnapper/robbers, and were generally supportive of their captors.

This certainly seemed like a curious outcome. We would have expected that the kidnapped victims would be upset and likely quite angry toward their kidnappers, maybe even wanting some kind of extensive revenge or at least demonstrative punishment for the crime committed. The local police brought in an expert psychiatrist/criminologist that said it was an example of brainwashing. A name arose of calling it the Stockholm Syndrome and it seems to have stuck ever since.

It is characterized as usually involving a bond developing between the hostages and the captors. The hostages might start out as rightfully hostile toward the captors, and then gradually shift toward having positive feelings toward them. This often slowly emerges during the period of captivity and is not usually instantaneous.

After getting out of captivity, the hostages might continue to retain the sense of positive bond. At first, the bonding often is quite high, and then dissipates over time. Ultimately, the hostages might someday change their minds and begin to have more pronounced negative feelings toward the captors. This all depends on a number of factors, such as the treatment of the hostages during the captivity portion, the interaction with their captors afterward, and so on.

If you carefully consider the phenomena, it might not seem particularly strange that during captivity the hostages might bond with their captors. One could say that this is a coping mechanism. It might increase your odds of survival. It might also be a means to mentally escape the reality of the situation. It could also be a kind of personal acquiescence to the situation and especially if you believe that you might not ever escape. Various psychological explanations are possible.

What tends to really puzzle outsiders is that after captivity the hostages would continue to retain that positive bond. It would seem that if you gained your freedom, and you were no longer under the belief that you had no other choices for pure survival purposes, you would pretty quickly bounce back with rage or some other similar reaction. We'd all allow that maybe for the first few minutes or hours after getting out of captivity that you might still be mired in what had occurred, but after days or even weeks or months, we'd assume that the hostages would recalibrate mentally and no longer have that false bonding muddled in their minds.

Some might say that the after-effect lasts because the hostage maybe wants to self-justify the earlier bonding. In other words, if you bonded during captivity, maybe afterward you would be embarrassed to admit it was a mistake, so you keep it going to try and show that it all made sense all along. Another explanation is that the person is so brainwashed at the time of captivity that it remains nearly permanently affixed in their psyche. There are lots of theories about this. No one explanation seems to be the all-purpose way to rationalize it.

Some object to the references about the Stockholm Syndrome and believe that it has become a kind of scapegoat to explain all sorts of unusual psychological situations. Some say it has been watered down due to overuse. Some say it never had a crisp definition to start with and has become a popularized item that lacks bona fide professional psychological bases and uses. Some try to create variants by renaming it to a local situation like say the Los Angeles Syndrome or the Piccadilly Square Syndrome.

Lately, some have been referring to a Tech Stockholm Syndrome, also called the High-Tech Stockholm Syndrome. Admittedly, it's a handy kind of reference paradigm that most people seem to know enough about that it can get their attention and interest. Allow me to explain it's use in the context of high-tech innovations.

Which brings us to the next point, namely, what does this have to do with AI self-driving cars?

At the Cybernetic AI Self-Driving Car Institute, we are developing AI software for self-driving cars. As part of that effort, we're also keenly interested in the trial tests of AI self-driving cars.

Google's Waymo has one of the most well-publicized of the trial tests of AI self-driving cars. They have for example been using a selected area of Phoenix, Arizona that involves having everyday people making use of the Waymo self-driving cars. This is being done as a kind of experiment, or maybe you'd prefer to call it a Proof Of Concept (POC), or a pilot, or a test, or a trial run, or whatever. Cleverly, Waymo calls it the "Early Rider Program" and the participants are Early Riders. The naming seems to bring forth imaginary of mavericks, those that dare to be first, and it provides an obviously upbeat way to portray the program (reminiscent of the movie Easy Rider and the freewheeling imagery of motorcyclists).

Let's clarify that these trial runs are not randomly picking up people off the street. Even though these are genuinely public kinds of trial runs, the participants need to first apply to the program. Only those applicants then chosen by Waymo are then allowed to participate. You can say that it is open to anyone in the sense that anyone can apply. Merely pointing out that whatever selection criteria is used, it then becomes semi-selective out of the pool of whomever actually applies. This is in contrast to say having AI self-driving cars roaming around Phoenix and picking up anyone that happens to flag one down.

The stated purpose of the Early Rider Program is to provide an opportunity for residents in the Phoenix geographical area to have access to these AI self-driving cars and provide feedback about them. In that sense, you can imagine how exciting it might be to become a chosen participant. You could help shape not only how Waymo is making AI self-driving cars, but maybe the entire future of AI self-driving cars.

And, the bragging rights would be awesome, including at the time of your participation and afterward. Imagine that you want to impress a date, and tell them you'll swing over at 7:00 p.m. to take them to dinner. Lo and behold, you show-up in an AI self-driving car. Whoa, impressive! Or, some years from now, when presumably AI self-driving cars are everywhere, you chat with a stranger and mention that, yes, you were one of the original pioneers that helped shape AI self-driving cars. You act modestly as though it was no big deal, and when the person says that you were like Neil Armstrong or "Buzz" Aldrin, Jr., you smile and say that you were a bit of a risk taker in your early days.

Speaking of risks, how much risk are these participants taking on? According to reports, the trial runs have had a back-up human driver from Waymo in the cars, thus, presumably, there's a licensed driver ready to takeover if needed. Presumably, this is not just any licensed driver, but one trained to keep their attention to the self-driving car and that is ready to step into the driving task when so needed. This definitely is intended to reduce the risks of the AI self-driving car going awry. But, this is also not necessarily a risk-free kind of ride, since there are numerous issues of having a so-called back-up driver and trying to co-share the driving task.

In quick recap, a trial run of this nature consists of vendor selected people in a pre-determined geographical area that are asked to participate in a kind of real-world experiment involving having AI self-driving cars transport them, doing so from time-to-time, as determined by the vendor. It's quite a bit different than having people come to a closed tracks or proving grounds to do trial runs, and so in that sense this is a bolder and more illuminating way to presumably get insightful feedback about AI self-driving cars.

One criticism is that these are indeed vendor selected participants, meaning that the auto maker or tech firm has chosen the people that are participating. Suppose there is some kind of purposeful selection criteria that is weaning out certain kinds of people, or maybe a subliminal selection bias, in which case, whatever is learned during these trial runs is lopsided. It doesn't presumably cover the full gamut of people. Will the result be an AI self-driving car that has certain kinds of biases and those biases will be reflected in what AI self-driving cars do and how they behave?

Another reported aspect is that the participants in such trial runs are required to sign NDA's (Non-Disclosure Agreements). This presumably restricts the participants from freely commenting to the public at large about their experiences of riding in these AI self-driving cars. You can certainly empathize with the auto maker or tech firm that they want to keep the participants somewhat under-wraps about their newly emerging AI self-driving cars. Imagine if a participant makes an off-hand remark that they hate the thing and no one should ever ride in one. This could be a completely unfair and baseless statement, which would appear to have credence simply because the person was a participant in the trial runs.

There could also be proprietary elements underlying the AI self-driving cars that could be blurted out by a participant and undermine the secrecy of the Intellectual Property (IP) of the vendor. Right now, the AI self-driving car companies are in a fierce battle to see who can achieve this moonshot first. There is already a lot of sneaking around to find out what other firms are doing. There's a potential treasure trove that you might be able to get a participant to unwittingly divulge.

There are idealists that think the auto makers and tech firms should not restrict the participants in any manner whatsoever. They argue that it is important for the public to know what these participants feel about AI self-driving cars. Good or bad. Right or wrong. Blemishes or not. It is for the good of the public overall to know what the participants have to say.

Furthermore, they would likely claim that it will help the other auto makers and tech firms too. In other words, if you believe that AI self-driving cars provide great benefits to society, the sooner we get there, the better for all of society. Thus, the more that the auto makers and tech firms share with each other, the sooner the benefits will emerge.

To some degree, the participants in these kinds of trial runs are periodically being allowed to say something about their experiences. You'll see a quote in this newspaper article or that magazine, or on this blog or on some social media site. Usually, it is a very carefully crafted indication, or at least one that has been vetted and approved for release by the auto maker or tech firm. It is rarely a fully off-the-cuff, anything-you-want-to-say utterance. This is again as a result of the NDA, and the auto maker or tech firm wanting to try and shape the public perception of the matter.

You can imagine that if rocket makers tried to make rockets, and if their trial runs had issues, it could become a public relations nightmare if the tiniest imperfections were made known and then potentially blown out of proportion. This actually does happen. Companies trying to create some new technology will at times get clobbered by the fact that it isn't working right, and yet they are aware that it is not yet ready for prime time, and hence their desire to run trials first.

But, if the trials become the focus of attention, and if only having complete perfection is the public criteria (even during the trial runs), the trials really serve no useful purpose, since you would need to hold back from doing any trials at all, until the system was perfected anyway.

It's kind of a Catch-22.

Let's though shift our attention to something else, but related to this whole topic.

At some of my recent presentations at industry conferences, I've been asked about some of the comments that participants in these trial runs have been saying so far. The comments are usually quite glowing. Even if there is a mention of something that went awry, the participants seem to then explain it away and the whole thing seems just peachy.

For example, a participant that reported an AI self-driving car that got somewhat lost in a mall parking lot trying to get to the rider's desired destination, and later on the AI developers adjusted the system to then instead go to a designated drop-off point. This is a lighthearted tale. No one was hurt, no apparent concern, other than maybe some excess time spent waiting for the AI self-driving car to find the proper spot. Plus, it was later fixed anyway.

Others with a more critical eye question these kinds of stories. Shouldn't we be concerned that the AI system wasn't able to better navigate the mall parking lot? Maybe there are other locations that it would have problems with too? Shouldn't we be concerned that the AI system itself wasn't able to make a correction, and that instead it required human intervention by the developers? If AI self-driving cars aren't going to be self-corrective, it seems to undermine what we are expecting of Machine Learning and the abilities of the AI for self-driving cars? And so on.

In any case, here's the question that I sometimes get asked – are these participants suffering from a Tech Stockholm Syndrome?

You might have wondered how I was going to connect the beginning of this piece that discussed the Stockholm Syndrome with the aspects of AI self-driving cars. Well, now you know.

There are some that seem to be concerned that the apparently whitewashed commentary being provided by the trial run participants might be a form of Stockholm Syndrome. Maybe the participants are being "brainwashed" into believing that the AI self-driving cars are fine and dandy. Perhaps this is coming out of then not by their own freewill, but by the droning of it into their heads.

I'll admit that I was a bit taken aback the first time I was asked this question. I believe my answer was, say what?

After some reflective thought, I pointed out that the "Stockholm Syndrome" is perhaps a misapplication in this case. The commonly accepted notion of the Stockholm Syndrome is that you have some kind of hostages and some kind of captors. I dare say, it doesn't seem like these trial run participants are hostages. They voluntarily agreed to participate. They put themselves forth to become participants. They weren't grabbed up in the cover of darkness and thrown into AI self-driving cars.

So, I reject the notion that you can somehow compare these trial runs with a hostage-captor scenario. The comparison might seem appetizing, especially if you are someone averse to the trial runs, or at least how you believe the trial runs are being run. It also has a clever stickiness to it, meaning that it could stick with the trial runs because it kind of sounds applicable on a surface basis.

Suppose I am going to create a new kind of ice cream. I ask for volunteers to taste it. Those that are volunteering are presumably already predisposed to liking ice cream. I select volunteers that are passionate about ice cream and really care for it. I then have them start tasting the ice cream. They like it, and it's a flavor and type they've never before had a chance to try. They are excited to be one of the first. They also believe they are shaping the future of ice cream for us all.

If I did that, I think we'd likely expect that the participants are going to generally have glowing comments about the ice cream trial. They might even suppress some of the not so good aspects, especially if we right away modified the flavors based on their feedback. After the trial runs are over, suppose the ice cream goes into mass production. I would anticipate that the original volunteers are likely to continue to say that the ice cream was great.

Does this mean that they are suffering from the Stockholm Syndrome? Just because they bonded in a positive way, and kept that positive bonding later on? I think that strips out an essence of the Stockholm Syndrome, the hostage part of things. The mistreatment part of things. The analogy or metaphor falls apart due to a key linking element that is not there.

During these trial runs of these emerging AI self-driving cars, if some of the participants get injured or killed due to the AI self-driving car, I'd be pretty shocked if that got covered up. I think we'd all know about it. One way or another, it would leak out. There would likely be lawsuits filed. Someone would leak it. An inquisitive reporter would find out about it. An anonymous tip would get posted on a blog. Etc.

I mention this aspect because for those that are concerned about the positive commentary to-date about these trial runs, I'm suggesting that if there is something really amiss, I think it will become known. In spite of the assertion that the participants are brainwashed, I doubt that the brainwashing could be that good that it would curtail a reveal about something systematically wrong and life threatening.

Overall, here's my key thoughts on this matter:

- Trial runs are a generally good thing for progress on AI self-driving cars

- Auto makers and tech firms need to remain vigilant to do these trial runs safely

- Participants might be somewhat muted about things that go awry, but this does not seem overly worrisome

- Participants will likely be reporting upbeat aspects, which we should consider and also at times take with a bit of salt

- Calamities during the trial runs are likely to get leaked out and so the public will not be in the dark

- It is understandable why there are various controls related to the release of info about the trial runs

- There does not seem to be any conspiratorial concerns on this (I'll add "as yet" for those that holdout for a conspiracy)

- Trying to say this is a Stockholm Syndrome seems to be an overreach and though seemingly on the surface appearing to be applicable, it is actually a misapplied notion and we should reject its use in this case

I suppose you might assert that maybe I've been taken hostage by the auto makers and tech firms, and I'm now suffering from the Tech Stockholm Syndrome. I say that with obviously a touch of humor. That being said, I don't want to downgrade or undermine the genuine use of the Stockholm Syndrome as a potential paradigm when applicable, so let's keep it in the toolbox for other needier and more relevant occasions, shall we.

CHAPTER 7

PARALYSIS AND
AI SELF-DRIVING CARS

CHAPTER 7

PARALYSIS AND
AI SELF-DRIVING CARS

I was in the woods with my family one day and it was getting towards nightfall. We were up on a mountain that was only reachable via an aerial tram. We had been forewarned several times by the tram operator as we came up for our outdoors romp that we had to get back to the tramway by sunset or we would be stranded up there for the night. It was just a simple day hike for us and so we had not packed any camping gear. I realize this sounds like a story by someone that later regrets they had not brought their overnight gear, but in this case, we really genuinely were determined not to be there at night time, I swear it.

Anyway, we started to hike back toward the tramway with plenty of time to spare and could well gauge how much sunlight we had left. The kids were enjoying the trip and there was a smattering of silvery snow on the ground. It was cold enough to have lightweight winter jackets on, but not so cold that you could see your breath. That being said, the temperature was dropping rapidly as darkness neared. We gradually picked up the pace and opted to move along more stridently, rather than stopping to look at every majestic tree and fallen pinecone.

Just as the tramway came into our sight, which was like reaching the pot of gold at the end of the rainbow, we also sighted something else that was at the opposite extreme of delight, a wolf. Turns out that a full-grown wolf had edged out of the woods onto the path that led to the tramway. He was facing us. We were facing him. I had no provision to be able to fight off the wolf, since I merely had the clothes on my back and nothing more. I was leading the way on this path and so saw the wolf before the rest of the family did so.

I signaled to my family to come to a stop. They at first thought I was kidding around, but they could see the seriousness and sternness of my facial expression. I whispered at them to quit goofing around and just stand still. The kids were very young, and so they were both frightened and yet also "excited" that something unusual was happening (I suppose if I was really brave, I would have wrestled with the wolf, right there in front of the kids, what a mountain man I would have been!).

Anyway, I was trying not to take my eyes off the wolf. Some say that you should stare down a wild animal, others say don't make direct eye contact. It's also said that it can be contextually based, as to the nature of the animal and the circumstance involved.

I knew this much, I wanted to know where the wolf was. Would it dart towards us? Would it meander? Would it quietly go back into the woods? Were there more wolves and this was just one of them? Was there an entire wolf pack surrounding us and this was the first one to show itself? If I yelled, would it scare off the wolf? If I yelled, would it instead cause the wolf to attack? Why would a wolf come this close to the tram station? Was it a domesticated kind of wolf that was used to being around people? Etc.

The rest of the family was watching me and watching the wolf. We were all standing still, including the wolf. It was some kind of momentary standoff. The kids were squirming but generally as still as young children can be. I was concerned that even trying to talk about the wolf and the situation might somehow spark the wolf into action. We all remained silent. In the woods. On a mountain. Nearing sunset.

With no one else left around.

I didn't see anyone yet at the tram station. One thought was that if we all just stayed frozen in position, maybe the tram was on its way up for the last haul of the day, and when it arrived the wolf would dart away. Even if the tram arrived and we were all still stationary, I figured we were close enough to the tram station that we might be able to get the attention of the tram operator. Hopefully, the tram operator was prepared for and used to having wolfs up in this area, and would know what to do.

You could say I was paralyzed.

Of course, I wasn't paralyzed in the sense that my arms weren't broken or my legs were not working. I was fine physically. We all were. I'd dare say the wolf looked to be in good shape too. We were paralyzed in the manner of none of us moving, and none of us yet willing to make a move. It was a situation in which we were paralyzed in place, unmoving, and "frozen" without any as yet identifiable viable move to best undertake. Nor was I paralyzed in fear. Sometimes you lose your wits and become paralyzed. In this case, I had my wits, I had my fitness.

I'd like to think that the wolf was also looking us over and mulling over the same kinds of thoughts we were having. Are those humans going to attack? Do they have food? Are they themselves food worthwhile to try and obtain? Will other humans come to their aid? Do they have a gun or other weapon? Are there more humans hidden in the woods? I realize that the wolf maybe wasn't playing a game of chess with us, but in some manner, even if simplistic, it sure seemed like it too was trying to size up the situation and determine what to do next.

I refer to this as being "paralyzed." If you are uncomfortable that I use the word paralysis, which I realize many believe should only be used when you are truly physically debilitated, I can use instead the word pseudo-paralysis if that's more palatable to you. Suppose we do this, for the rest of this discussion, whenever you see me use the word paralysis, substitute instead the word pseudo-paralysis. Hope that's OK with you all.

In a moment, you'll grasp why I've discussed the topic of paralysis and led you to a juncture of considering paralysis as a circumstance involving coming to a halt, being faced with seemingly difficult choices of what to do next, and remaining in a stopped position for some length of time.

I'll quickly finish the story since I am assuming you are on the edge of your seat.

I didn't want us to back-up since I thought it might cause the wolf to think we were weak and by retreating maybe it would come after us. I didn't want to go forward because I thought it would be perceived as an attacking threat. I didn't want to go sideways which would have led us into the woods and I figured that being among the trees would be more to the advantage of a cunning wolf than us daytrip humans. Seemed like quite a stalemate. Fortunately, the wolf apparently grew tired of the standoff, and it wandered back into the woods. We moved quickly over to the tram station and with great relief got onto the tram once it arrived.

What does this have to do with AI self-driving cars?

At the Cybernetic AI Self-Driving Car Institute, we are developing AI software for self-driving cars. This also includes considering scenarios in which the self-driving car might find itself becoming pseudo-paralyzed due to a predicament or particular situation.

First, let me clarify that I am not referring to a circumstance involving the self-driving car having a malfunction. Similar to my story, I am referring to a situation for which the AI has to make a decision about what way to go, and there doesn't seem to be a viable choice at hand. This is different than having a physical ailment of some kind. Just as I was physically able to move around while facing the wolf, I was "paralyzed" with respect to the situation and what action to take. For the moment, taking no action seemed prudent.

There will be circumstances that an AI self-driving car freezes up due to some kind of potential malfunction, but that's a different topic than this one about paralysis aspects. Herein, let's assume that the AI self-driving car is fully able and can go forwards, backwards, turn, and the like.

You might be wondering what kind of a situation could arise then that would cause a functioning AI self-driving to become pseudo-paralyzed.

One of the most famous examples involves the early days of AI self-driving cars and their actions when coming to a four-way stop. An AI self-driving car arrived at a four-way stop sign just as other cars did. The other cars were driven by humans. Even though the proper approach would normally be that whichever car arrives first then goes forward first, the other human driven cars weren't necessarily abiding by this. It's a dog eat dog world, and I'm sure you've had other drivers that have opted to force themselves forward and abridge your "right" to go ahead before they do.

The AI self-driving car kept waiting for the other cars to come to a full and proper halt. Those other cars kept doing the infamous rolling stop. Each time that the AI self-driving car perceived that maybe it could start to go, one of the other cars moved forward, which then caused the AI to bring the self-driving car to a halt. You might have seen a teenage novice driver get themselves into a similar bind. They sit at the stop sign, politely waiting for their turn, which never seems to arrive.

You could say that this is a form of paralysis. Admittedly, the AI self-driving car was fully able to drive forward. It could even go in reverse. It was a fully functioning car. The predicament or circumstance was that it was trying to abide by the laws of driving, and it was trying to avoid a potential accident with any other car. Under that set of circumstances, it become pseudo-paralyzed. Perhaps you can see now how my story about being in the woods and spotting the wolf relates to this – I was fully able to move, but the situation seemed to preclude doing so.

There's another example of an AI self-driving car paralysis that was recently reported about the real-world trials being undertaken by Waymo in Phoenix, Arizona. Reportedly, one of their AI self-driving cars drove to the school of a family that was participating in the trial runs and waited for the school children to be released from the school. You've maybe done this or seen this before, wherein cars sit waiting for the bell to ring and the school children to come flying out of the classrooms, and kids will pile into the waiting cars.

If you've not had an opportunity to be a human driver in the school setting of this kind, I assure you that it can be one of the most memorable times of your driving career (well, maybe not fondly memorable!).

I used to endure the same situation when I was picking up my children from school. When the cars first arrived to the school, prior to the bell ringing, it is relatively quiet and everyone jockeys to find a place to temporarily park. Some leave their motor running; some turn off the car. Some read a book while waiting, some watch the school intently. Some actually get out of their cars, as though it is a taxi line at the airport, and converse with other fellow parents waiting likewise to pick-up their children.

That first part of the effort is relatively easy. The main aspect is that you need to be careful about where you park, and that you don't cut-off someone else or disturb what has become a kind of daily ritual with everyone seemingly knowing the "rules" about where to park and wait. It can be an unavoidable death sentence to anyone that decides to squeeze their car in front of everyone else that has already been waiting for the last twenty minutes or so. I'm sure the person would be dragged out of their car and beaten senseless.

Well, the real excitement happens when the kids burst out of the classrooms. Everyone starts their car engines as though it is the start of an Indy car race. The kids weave in and out of the parked cars to get to their parent's car. Some kids take their time and end-up blocking other cars. Some kids run to their designated car but meanwhile get confused and maybe bounce off someone else's car. The parents will try to maneuver their car closer toward their child. It becomes a free-for-all. Measured chaos, or worse.

Well, apparently, an AI self-driving car from Waymo found itself in such a situation. The AI self-driving car became pseudo-paralyzed. Whichever way it might go, there were nearby objects. Other cars were blocking it. Children were blocking it. Probably other parents were walking around trying to help the children, and they were blocking it too. No means to move. Notice that the AI self-driving car was fully functioning, and it could have driven in any desired direction, but the situation precluded doing so.

If the AI self-driving car had tried to move forward, it might have hit someone or something. If it tried to back-up, it might have hit someone or something. If it turned to the left or turned to the right, it might have hit someone or something. All told, it was a kind of stalemate. Just like with the wolf, it became a wait and see what will happen in the environment that might allow for breaking out of the stalemate.

You might be saying that the AI was just trying to be cautious. It could have run over the children or parents; it could have rammed into the other cars. Let's concede that indeed it could have moved if it intended to do so. Fortunately, the AI was well-programmed enough that it realized those were not seemingly viable options in this case. The need to avoid hitting these surrounding objects had kept the self-driving car from moving.

One current criticism of AI self-driving cars is that they are perhaps overly cautious. They are actually skittish, which can be a limiting factor when driving a car. If you've seen a teenage novice driver trying to drive in a busy mall parking lot, you might know what I mean by skittish. The novice won't drive down a parking lane because there are people walking to and fro. There are cars backing up. There are cars waiting in the parking lane and it becomes dicey to squeeze around them.

Do we want our AI self-driving cars to be skittish? This can be a "safe" way to drive, one might argue, but it also means that there will be lots of real-world driving situations that will inhibit the self-driving car and it will become possibly paralyzed. Imagine the frustration of other human drivers at the skittishly driven car – they honk their horn, and can be blocked by the paralyzed car and unable themselves to move along. Pedestrians can be confused too. Is that self-driving car going to move or not move?

There are some that even have been playing tricks on AI self-driving cars. You can get some of the AI self-driving cars to come to a halt, simply by standing at the curb and waving your arms frantically as it gets close to you, while it is driving down the street. The AI self-driving car will likely slow down, and in some cases even come to a halt. This is partially because the AI developers have opted to establish a kind of protective virtual bubble around the self-driving car. If there is anything that nears the bubble or comes into the bubble, there's a chance that the self-driving car will hit it, so the safest bet by the AI programmers seems to be have the self-driving car slow down or come to a stop.

This is considered an essential deployment of the "first, do no harm" principle of the AI being developed by most of the auto makers and tech firms. Driving the car is essential, but harming people or destroying things is a big no-no. Thus, make the protective virtual bubble as large and encompassing as you can. Don't scrimp on the magnitude of the bubble. Make the bubble big so as to reduce the risks of causing injury or death to the smallest amount that you can.

Humans don't typically drive this way. Humans have seemed to be able to refine their driving practices to take things to a much closer margin. I realize you might say that's why there are car accidents and people that get run over by cars. True. But, on the balance, there seems to have been a "societal dance" that by-and-large has been established of driving our cars and doing so within an inch of others, and meanwhile most of the time there aren't injuries and deaths.

I recently went to a baseball game and parked in a very busy parking lot. The entire time in the parking lot, while driving around to find a parking spot, people were not only super close to my car, many people at times touched my car (transgressions!). When I finally found an open spot, I pulled into it, and was within a scant inch or so of the cars on either side.

Most of the AI self-driving cars would become "paralyzed" with that kind of closeness. There's going to be a delicate ratcheting up of the risk aspects to allow for closer movement. Human occupants in an AI self-driving car aren't going to be satisfied that their AI self-driving car has come to a halt and is going to wait say thirty minutes for everyone else in a parking lot to get into or out of their cars and clear out the lot before the AI will instruct the self-driving car to move again. We're going to expect that the AI can drive like a human can, which means being able to navigate these kinds of situations.

In the case of the AI self-driving car among the school children, what should the AI have done?

Let's first consider the four-way stop sign scenario. In that situation, the AI self-driving car likely should have played chicken with the other human driven cars and opted to move forward, showcasing that it was wanting to move along. The other human driven cars would inevitably have backed-down and allow the AI self-driving car to go ahead. It was the omission of a clear cut indication that the AI self-driving car was going to "aggressively" make its move that the other human driven cars figured they would just outdo or outrun it.

Some would say that if there's a politeness meter related to the AI, it's time to move the needle towards the impolite side of things. Human drivers can be quite impolite. They get used to other drivers being the same way. Therefore, if they see a polite driver, they figure the driver is a sheep. It is worthwhile to be the fox and treat the sheep like sheep, so the impolite driver figures. Right now, AI self-driving cars are perceived as the meek sheep. Easy to exploit.

Does this imply that the AI self-driving car should run amuck? Should it barrel down a street? Should it try to take possession of the roadway and make it clear that is it the king of the traffic? No, I don't think anyone is suggesting this, at least not now.

Also, let's be frank, it's harder to go the impolite route when right now all eyes are on AI self-driving cars and how they are driving.

The moment an AI self-driving car bumps or harms a human, or scrapes against another car, this is going to be magnified a thousand fold as a reason why AI self-driving cars are to not be trusted. Suppose a human driver was on probation for having driven badly, and they were then on-notice that any tiny misdeed would have their license get revoked. Many of the AI developers are worried that the same thing is going to happen with the initial emergence of AI self-driving cars.

Let's revisit the school children and picking up the kids at school. What do the parents do when they want to drive out of the morass of cars and kids? They usually edge forward, which is a signal to the other cars and the kids to get out of the way. This generally seems to work. It's almost like being amongst a herd and you kind of make your own pathway while in the middle of the herd.

Rather than being paralyzed, these human drivers "push" their way out of the situation. Sure, some of them are momentarily "paralyzed" but they are overtly making their way through the crowded scene. This is somewhat akin to the practice suggested to alleviate the four-way stop paralysis too.

This brings up the importance of the time factor when referring to this pseudo-paralysis.

How much time has to be spent sitting still to declare a paralysis? This is a hard thing to quantify across all circumstances and situations. If I'm in my car and waiting at a red light, I'll need to do so for the time it takes for the light to turn green. Are me and my car paralyzed? I don't think so. I'd suggest that we would all agree this is not quite the circumstance that we're referring to when we discuss the paralyzed self-driving car.

Returning to the school children situation, suppose the AI self-driving car opts to be more aggressive. In doing so, it might bump into a child, or bump into another car. Obviously, that's not desirable. You could say that the human parents could also though have done the same thing, they could have bumped into a child or bumped into a car. Fortunately, most of the time, they don't. This is the kind of delicate maneuvering that a true AI self-driving car should strive to achieve.

Let's consider other scenarios that might lead to paralysis of an AI self-driving car, and consider what to do about it.

The AI self-driving car is driving along an open highway. A group of motorcyclists gradually come up to where the AI self-driving car is driving along. It's doing 55 miles per hour. The motorcyclists were doing 80 miles per hour to catch-up with the AI self-driving car. Upon reaching the AI self-driving car, they all slow down to 55 miles per hour. They completely surround the AI self-driving car. What should the AI self-driving car do?

You've maybe seen YouTube videos of groups of motorcyclists that have done this to human drivers. Presumably, you would just keep driving and try to avoid a confrontation. Suppose though that the motorcyclists start to slow their speed. The AI self-driving car will presumably need to slow down, else it will hit the motorcyclists ahead of it, and it cannot change lanes because the motorcyclists are there too. Now what?

If you say that the AI self-driving car should slow down, it then takes us to the next step, imagine that the motorcyclists are going to gradually come to a halt. They could essentially get the AI self-driving car to come to a halt, doing so on an open highway. Is that safe? Would you, the human occupants, inside the AI self-driving car want that to happen? Maybe you feel that the motorcyclists are trying to threaten you, and they are readily using the AI to let it happen.

Here's another similar kind of scenario. You are in an AI self-driving car. Unluckily for you, you've wandered into an area that has a riot erupting. The AI self-driving car has come to a halt, paralyzed, because there are rioters completely surrounding the self-driving car. The rioters bang on the self-driving car and are aiming to get in and harm you. What should the AI self-driving car do?

Some would say that the AI self-driving car should not allow itself to get into such a situation. That's not much of a helpful answer. Sure, if there's an obvious situation that you can avoid, it would be handy if the AI could possibly predict a situation and avoid it. In the case of the school children, it's reportedly been indicated that the AI developers advised that the AI self-driving car not go into the muddled area to pick-up the children, and instead find a less crowded area to park and wait. Though this seems perhaps sensible, I'd suggest it has downsides, such as maybe causing the children to walk further to get to the car, increasing their chances of getting hit or other calamity occur. Also, notably, it was not a solution devised by the AI, but instead relied upon the AI developers to suggest or devise.

The point being that having a skittish AI self-driving car that has to avoid situations that can lead to paralysis is certainly something to keep in mind, but it doesn't seem to fully address the problem. Also, we'd prefer that the AI is able to "reason" about what to do, rather than hoping or betting that the AI developers can find a workaround. In the real-world, the AI self-driving car has to do what a human driver might do, and not necessarily be able to "phone a friend" to get out of a jam.

That being said, it is vital too that whenever AI self-driving cars find themselves in a paralyzing situation, the experience can be shared with other AI self-driving cars. Most of the auto makers and tech firms have setup a cloud-based system to allow for data collection and machine learning for their line of self-driving cars, known as OTA (Over The Air) capabilities. We find that having these particular kinds of experiences shared into the cloud can be handy as a means of getting others of the AI self-driving cars to avoid like situations or at least have some possibilities of what to do when such a circumstance arises.

Another form of sharing among AI self-driving cars involves V2V (vehicle to vehicle communications). This would be handy when an AI self-driving car has discovered a paralyzing situation, and it might forewarn other nearby AI self-driving cars about it. Besides perhaps staying away from the situation so as to avoid getting into a paralyzing predicament, it might also be possible that multiple AI self-driving cars might come to each other's aid, and find a means to jointly get out of the situation. This could make use of swarm intelligence.

There are other coping strategies for the AI self-driving car. It could potentially interact with the human occupants and maybe jointly identify a means to get out of the paralysis situation. This could be good, or it could be bad. If the human occupant offers helpful insights, it could be good. If the human occupants say something like run them all down, it could be problematic as a solution to be considered viable by the AI system.

In quick recap:

- Try to avoid paralyzing situations, if feasible

- Seek to learn from paralyzing situations, doing so via OTA and cloud-based machine learning

- Be able to recognize when a paralyzing situation is arising

- Once in a paralysis, be considering ways out of it

- Keep watch of the clock to gauge how long it is lasting

- Tendency toward impoliteness or aggressiveness as a possible paralysis buster

- Reduce the bubble size but simultaneously increase the driving capability

- Potentially confer with other AI self-driving cars via V2V about such situations

- Other

Currently, most of the auto makers and tech firms aren't giving much consideration to the paralysis predicament. They tend to consider this to be an "edge" problem (one that is not at the core of the driving task per se). Many AI developers tell me that if the AI self-driving car has to wait until the school children disperse or the baseball parking lot becomes empty, it's fine as a driving strategy, and meanwhile the human occupants can be enjoying themselves in the car during the waiting time. I don't think this is reasonable, and furthermore it ignores the often adverse consequent aspects of having the self-driving car being in the paralyzed state.

It's time to make sure AI self-driving cars are able to cope with potentially paralyzing situations.

There is a famous saying that often times people fail at a task due to analysis paralysis. They over-analyze a situation and thus get stuck in doing nothing. You might claim that when I was in the woods and facing the wolf, I was over-thinking things and had analysis paralysis. I don't believe so. I was doing analysis and had ascertained that no action seemed to be the best course of action, for the moment, and remained alert and ready to take action, when action seemed suitable.

In the case of pseudo-paralysis for AI self-driving cars that I've been depicting here, I'm not herein been focusing on instances where the AI self-driving cars get themselves into an analysis infinite loop and suffer analysis paralysis. Instead the situation itself is causing the paralysis, as dictated by the desire to avoid injuring others, and so the need to remain alert and ready for making a move whenever suitable. That's the kind of paralysis we can overcome with better AI.

CHAPTER 8
UGLY ZONES
AND
AI SELF-DRIVING CARS

CHAPTER 8

UGLY ZONES
AND AI SELF-DRIVING CARS

Is he a man or a machine? That was asked about Francesco Molinari when he recently won the 2018 Open Golf Championship and earned himself nearly $2 million in prize money. It was his first major golf victory and it was the first time that the now 147th annual golf tournament was won by an Italian (there was a lot of celebrating in Italy!).

How did he achieve the win?

You could say that it was years upon years of other golf competitions and smaller wins that led to this big win. You could say it was maybe the weather conditions and the mood and skills of the other golfers at the tournament that converged to let him be the best on that particular occasion. You could say it was random chance. You could say that he had a lucky charm.

Would you be willing to say it was due to practice?

As they famous joke goes, how do you get to Carnegie Hall – via practice, practice, practice. Francesco is known for being a slave to practicing. Of course, the odds are that many of the other golfers there had put in as many hours practicing as he has. It stands to reason that golfers at that level of play are practicing all of the time, day and night. They likely dream about golf. They likely are mentally playing golf when they eat lunch or dinner. It's an all-consuming passion for most of them.

If they are all practicing about the same amount of the time, perhaps the nature of how they practice might account for some of the differences in their playing levels. Just because I say that I practice, it doesn't indicate in what manner I practice. For almost any kind of practices, you can take a varied approach to how you practice.

I used to play tennis when I was in college. My practices often involved hitting tennis balls against a wall for hours on end. When I could find someone to play against, I'd certainly do a practice game, but at other times it was solo practicing that took place. Is the potential outcome of the solo practicing as good as doing actual practice games? You can debate the matter. The practice games are certainly more akin to what will occur when playing a match game, and so it seems logical that the practice game is a better form of practice. On the other hand, the repetition of hitting hundreds of times back-and-forth against a wall does build-up your arm and body in a manner that a practice game cannot.

Francesco realized about two years ago that he needed to do something to boost his golf game. He had been a professional golfer for more than a dozen years and had been an amateur champion before turning pro. But, he had not yet reached the top echelon of the winner's circle of professional players. Would it take some kind of voodoo magic to push him to the top? Did he have to make changes to how he perceived golf and played golf?

He opted to radically change his practice routines. He entered into the ugly zone.

For those of you familiar with the Twilight Zone (the old TV series), I suppose the ugly zone sounds somewhat like it. There's nothing too odd about the ugly zone though. The concept is relatively straightforward. When practicing any kind of skill, you are to do so with a maximum amount of pressure, perhaps even more so than what you'll experience during live competition play. The goal is to make practices as rough and tough as a real match. Maybe even more so.

When I used to help coach my son's Little League baseball team, we often had rather animated debates among the coaches and assistant coaches about whether the practices should be easy or hard. There were some coaches that said we should be easy on the kids and provide a supportive environment for them to learn baseball and hone their skills. It was about fun. It was about falling in love with the sport. We knew in contrast that the actual games would be pressure cookers, so the practices would hopefully serve as a means to inspire them towards becoming proficient baseball players.

If you've not been to a Little League baseball game, allow me to open your eyes. You've got the doting parents that want their kids to win no matter what it takes. Many hope that their child will someday become a big leaguer, getting the big paychecks and the big fame.

Some of the eager parents had a different but similarly high pressure perspective, namely they thought that winning was the key to life, and they didn't care that it was a baseball game per se. Instead, it was that their child needed to discover that winning is good and losing is bad. Period. It wasn't so important that the child was able to swing a bat -- what was really paramount was that you must win however you can achieve it – this includes maybe swinging a bat, or catching a fly ball, or tricking the opposing team, screaming at the other team, spitting on the other team, you name it (all's fair in love and war, and baseball).

Should the practices be like the games? Would it be better to have the boys experience the crazed high pressures of a real game during their practices, or would that distract them from the needed step-at-a-time of learning their craft? Maybe doing high pressure practices would make them emotionally upset and they would become disgruntled about playing the sport entirely. They'd also have no opportunity to try out new techniques. They'd be constantly under the gun, so to speak.

You'll find this anecdote amusing (or, maybe serious!). One of the coaches suggested that we setup loudspeakers at practice that would blare out the sounds of a typical game audience, including a recorded cacophony of loudmouthed spectators yelling and screaming, doing so during the practices (side note, we opted to not do that). This would help re-create the setting of actual games, apparently.

Anyway, there are some that philosophically believe that practices need to be conducted in a high pressure manner that aligns with the pressures encountered during competitive matches. Of course, maybe doing this with Little League kids is not the right audience. Perhaps we might say that this approach is more suitable to adults. Furthermore, adults that are already versed in their craft, rather than someone just starting out to gain a new skill.

Well, I realize that some of you that believe in the ugly zone approach will maybe disagree with me and my list of carve out exceptions, and you'll insist that the ugly zone is always applicable, regardless of age, skill level, etc. Fine, have it your way. Let's agree to disagree, and continue on, thanks.

Francesco shifted his practices two years ago into becoming near torture tests. His new coach embodied the ugly zone philosophy and emphasized that the frustration level had to be equal to a real game or possibly higher than a real game. The more annoyed that Francesco became with his coach, the more the coach knew he was doing something right in terms of making practices hard. Every practice golf shot was considered vital. No more of the traditional hitting golf balls with your clubs for mindless hours on end. Instead, all sorts of complicated shots and series of shots were devised for practices.

There you are on the putting green, practicing. You are 8 feet away from the hole. You try to make the putt, but miss the hole. It's practice, so you just shrug your shoulders, you try to figure out what went wrong, and you then casually setup to do the same shot again. Not so with the ugly zone. That 8-foot putt is for the golden trophy, every time. If you miss the hole, you are done for. You are a failure. You must take each and every putt with somber seriousness. If you happen to make the putt the first time, that's not good enough. Do it again. Indeed, do it five times in a row, flawlessly.

Some psychologists suggest that adding challenges to practices tends to boost the long-term impacts of the practices. It is often referred to as desirable difficulty. As mentioned earlier, you might perceive that this challenges factor should be for all of the practices and all of the time of the practices, or you might believe that it should be done in a more measured fashion, just for some of the practices and maybe for just some of the time of those practices.

Let's take a slightly different angle on this ugly zone notion.

Suppose you had practices that never were in the ugly zone. So far, I've mentioned the belief by some that the practices should always and exclusively be in the ugly zone. The opposite tack perhaps would be to never use the ugly zone approach at all. I've seen this happen in some contexts.

For example, I was helping a group of middle school students learn about robotics as they were getting ready for a robotics competition. A fellow mentor was purposely having them avoid encountering any problems while practicing writing code to program the robots for doing various tasks. I took him aside and gently pointed out that we ought to have the kids experience some issues or errors, so that they'd be ready during the live competition. He insisted that any kind of difficulty would mar their learning and rebuffed my suggestion. Sadly, things didn't go very well for them during the live competition and they were baffled as to what to do when their robots faltered.

So, I'd generally argue that you need some amount of ugly zone involved in practicing. I suppose that I'm the Goldilocks kind of practices person. It should be not too much ugly zone, and nor too little ugly zone. Just the right amount of ugly zone is the aim. And, crucially, having no ugly zone at all is likely an unfortunate and perhaps misguided omission that undermines the overall utility of the practices.

The ugly zone proponents contend that you need to learn how to think and act under pressure. They say that if you are the type of person that gets butterflies in your stomach during live competitions, you need to hone your skills so that instead of expunging the butterflies that you instead learn to shape them so they fly in a formation. Use the pressure to overcome your fears. Use the pressure as a kind of high octane juice. That's what the ugly zone is supposed to achieve.

What does this have to do with AI self-driving cars?

At the Cybernetic AI Self-Driving Car Institute, we are developing AI software for self-driving cars. In addition, we make use of a wide variety of techniques and one of those that we advocate is the use of the ugly zone.

Allow me to explain.

Many of the auto makers and tech firms that are making AI self-driving cars are doing testing in these ways:

- Use of simulations

- Use of proving grounds

- Use on public roads

When an AI self-driving car is being "tested" on public roads, this means it is being done in a relatively uncontrolled environment and that presumably just about anything can happen. On the one hand, this is good because there might be that "unexpected" aspect that arises and for which it is then handy to see how well the AI can respond to the matter. On the other hand, you might go hundreds, thousands, or millions of miles using the AI self-driving car and not encounter these plausible rare occasions at all, thus, in that sense, the AI self-driving car will not be tested readily on such facets.

There's also the rather obvious but worth stating point that doing "testing" of AI self-driving cars while on public roads is something of a dicey proposition. If the AI is unable to appropriately respond to something that occurs, the public at large could be endangered.

Suppose a man on a pogo stick suddenly appears in front of the AI self-driving car and the AI does not know what to do, and perhaps hits and injures the man – that's not good.

As I've mentioned many times, there are some AI developers that have an "egocentric" perspective about AI self-driving cars and seem to think that if someone does something "stupid" like pogoing in front of a self-driving car that they get what they deserve (this will doom the emergence AI self-driving cars, I assure you). There is also some sense of false security by many of the auto makers and tech firms that having a human back-up driver during public roadway testing is a sure way of avoiding any adverse incidents. This is quite a myth or misunderstanding, and there is still a bona fide chance that even with a human back-up driver that things can go awry for an AI self-driving car.

Another aspect of doing testing on public roadways is that it might be difficult to reproduce the instance of what happened. I mention this because trying to do Machine Learning (ML) via only one example of something is quite difficult to do. It would be handy to be able to undertake the situation a multitude of times in order to try and arrive at a "best" or at least better way to respond. I've stated in my industry speeches that we're suffering from a kind of irreproducibility in the AI self-driving car realm and for which inhibits or staggers potential progress.

As perhaps is evident, doing testing on public roadways has some disadvantages. That's why it is vital to also do testing via the other means possible, including using simulations and using proving grounds.

For simulations, you can presumably run the AI through zillions of scenarios. There's almost no limit to what you could try to test. The main constraint would be the computational cycles needed. Some auto makers and tech firms are even using supercomputers for their simulations, similar to how such high-powered computing is being used to gauge the impacts of climate change or other large-scale problems.

Not everyone though necessarily believes that the simulations are true to the real-world and thus the question is posed whether the AI reacting in a simulated environment is actually the same as it will react while on the roadways. If you are simulating climate change and your simulation is a bit off-base by estimates being made, this is likely Okay. But, if you are dealing with AI self-driving cars, which are multi-ton beasts that can produce instantaneous life-or-death consequences, a simulation that isn't true to the real-world does not give one a full sense of confidence in the results.

In essence, if I told you that I had an AI self-driving car that has successfully passed a simulation of over one-hundred million miles of car driving, albeit only in a computer-based simulation, and never been on an actual road, would you be happy to see it now placed into public use, or unhappy, or disturbed, or what? I think it's fair to say that you'd be concerned.

There's also the potential use of proving grounds. This is either private land or sometimes government land that is set aside for the purposes of testing AI self-driving cars. You could say that this is "better" than simulations because it has a real-world aspect to it. You could say that this is "better" than being on the public roadways since it is in an area that avoids potential harm to the general public. You'd though also need to admit that it is perhaps "less than" being on public roadways because of the constraints of the proving ground, and also that proving ground testing can be quite expensive and not allow for as many scenarios as you could do via simulation.

It seems apparent that you'd want to use a combination of simulations, proving grounds, and public roadways for testing of your AI self-driving car. Each approach has its own merits. Each approach has its own drawbacks. In combination, you can aim to get more kinds of testing that will hopefully lead to sounder AI self-driving cars.

Let's now revisit the ugly zone.

For real-world driving of an AI self-driving car, as mentioned earlier, the AI might go for many miles without ever encountering some really difficult driving situations. Any such instances would presumably occur by happenstance, if at all. With a providing ground, you can possibly setup the AI for having to cope with quite ugly situations. Same goes for the use of simulations.

Regrettably, there are some auto makers and tech firms that are not pushing their AI to the limits via the use of the proving grounds and nor the simulations. They seem to believe that the focus should be the "normal" conditions of driving.

For example, at a proving ground, the AI self-driving car is driving on a road and all of a sudden a woman pushing a baby stroller carriage starts to walk across the street (this is a stunt woman hired for this purpose, and the baby stroller is empty other than a fake doll). The AI self-driving car detects the motions and objects involved, i.e., the adult female and the stroller, and deftly swerves to avoid them. AI saves the day! Case closed, the AI is prepared for such a scenario.

This seems convincing as a test. You might mark-off on your checklist and claim that the AI can detect a person with a baby stroller and take the right kind of action to avoid a calamity.

Allow me to burst that bubble.

How many other cars were on the road with the AI self-driving car? In this case, none. Was there a car directly next to the AI self-driving car that would have been potentially in the way of the swerving action? Not in this case. Were there other pedestrians also trying to cross the street at the same time as the woman and the stroller? No, just the woman and the stroller. Were there any road signs warning about an upcoming hazard or perhaps any orange cones in the road due to roadway repairs being made? No.

And so on.

I think we would all feel a bit more confident in the testing of avoiding the woman with the baby stroller if we believed it was done in a more high-pressure situation. Imagine if the AI self-driving car had other cars all around it, boxing it in, and meanwhile there were lots of other pedestrians near to or approaching the self-driving car, and the road itself was a mess, and a lot of things were happening all at once. That's more telling about what the AI can cope with. Having a simplified, stripped down situation with an otherwise barren road, and just the woman and the stroller, does not seem like much of a test per se. It's not anything close to being an ugly zone.

Don't misunderstand my point. I'm fine with the stripped down test as one such test. But, if that's going to be the nature of the testing that's taking place, it would seem like there's no provision for the ugly zone. Recall that I earlier mentioned that having a practice without any kind of ugly zone would seem to be a practice that has a substantial omission and we ought to question the validity of the practice overall.

For AI self-driving cars, we should definitely have ugly zone testing (or, if you prefer, we can say "practices" rather than "testing"). Should you use only and always ugly zones? Well, as I mentioned previously, I'm an advocate for a measured amount of practice time for sometimes having ugly zones and sometimes not. My Goldilocks viewpoint is to have a combination of times with and without the ugly zones. But, however you allocate the time, there must be some amount of ugly zone practice.

Avoidance of using an ugly zone approach in undertaking practices for AI self-driving cars is a scary and understated form of practice and will pretty much "guarantee" the failure of AI self-driving cars in the real-world.

Per my framework, these are the key AI self-driving car driving tasks:

- Sensor data collection and interpretation
- Sensor fusion
- Virtual world model updating
- AI action planning
- Cars control commands issuance

The ugly zone is a means to see how well each of those AI elements are able to perform. Furthermore, you want to see how well they each individually work as a semi-independent component, along with how they work in concert together to drive the self-driving car. Therefore, the ugly zone needs to have a varied and myriad of aspects that will put "pressure" on each of the components.

You might wonder how you can "pressure" an AI system, since it's not like a human wherein you can pressure a human to get into a tizzy by throwing all sorts of things at them at once. Actually, in some ways, you can indeed pressure the AI system by doing likewise of what you'd do to a human, namely, pile-on as many things as you can, and see what the AI does. The internal timing of the AI system needs to be taxed to see that it can handle a multitude of simultaneous things happening on the roadway at the same time and in the same place.

We believe in the ugly zone approach for AI self-driving cars. Let's create as tough an environment as feasible so that once the AI self-driving car is on the public roadways, it's a piece of cake. True stress testing should be done "in the lab" and not wait until the AI self-driving car is in a public place and for which public harm can occur. Whether you want to put your own children into an ugly zone for their piano practices or for their art lessons, that's up to you. I think we can all agree that we'd believe more so in the potential of AI self-driving cars to be trustworthy on our streets if we knew that they had survived, learned from, and were adept at dealing with ugly zones. Go, ugly zones, go.

.

CHAPTER 9

RIDESHARING AND
AI SELF-DRIVING CARS

CHAPTER 9

RIDESHARING AND
AI SELF-DRIVING CARS

Stick to your knitting. That's a famous line and the implication is that you should do what you know best to do. It acts also as a warning to be wary of going beyond your knitting. If you step outside your zone, it could be dicey. It could be troubling. It could be disastrous.

There's also another interpretation. If you have a knitting, you ought to know what it is, and thus you can stick with it. In other words, if you don't even know what your knitting is, you likely have little chance or maybe a random chance of even sticking with it, since you didn't even know that it existed.

Why all this talk about knitting?

Because there is a myriad of firms deeply involved in AI self-driving cars and the question arises as to which of them are sticking to their knitting and which of them are not.

I'd dare say that we all would likely agree that any major auto maker has to be doing something substantial as it relates to AI self-driving cars. An auto maker is by definition a maker of automobiles. If you believe that the AI self-driving car will ultimately transform the landscape of cars as an industry and a marketplace, an auto maker would seem pretty foolish and blind to not be trying to anticipate and cope with that emergent radical change.

Last year, the Ford CEO Mark Fields was ousted and some analysts say it was to a great extent due to his seemingly lukewarm attitude and actions toward AI self-driving cars. It didn't seem to the marketplace that he was willing to move boldly into AI self-driving cars. Perception and reality are two important concepts. The perception by the marketplace is that auto makers must be doing something of substance about AI self-driving cars, even if the auto maker maybe has its doubts about AI self-driving cars. By doubts, I don't necessarily mean that the auto maker believes it cannot be achieved, it might be instead that they see it as a longer term proposition.

If you were the head of an auto maker, and if you believed that true AI self-driving cars are not likely for another decade or more, you might opt to spend the company's resources towards other more pressing matters right now. Most firms live from quarter to quarter, and maybe can do some form of 3 to 5 year planning for what's ahead. Confronted with limited resources and tough choices, you might be tempted to push off those things that seem like a remote chance of happening anytime soon, and use your efforts towards those in the nearer term that seem to matter.

This might seem prudent, except for the fact that the marketplace might have a different view on the topic. If there is a mania toward something, and it's in your line of business, and you seem to be ignoring it or discounting it, the odds are that the market will punish you. They will interpret your hesitations as an indicator of being stodgy, of being ignorant, of being ill-informed. It will be assumed that you are out to lunch. It will be assumed that you are going to let some disrupter step into your industry and transform it and wipe you out. Meanwhile, you stood around and just watched it happen. Bad on you.

Some liken the upcoming shift toward AI self-driving cars from conventional cars as similar to the shift from horse and carriage to the advent of the automobile. Sure, it took years to happen. But, meanwhile, further investing in those carriages and those horses is going to be interpreted as mired in the past. Via hindsight, we now know that the automobile did indeed overtake the horse and carriage.

You might argue that we don't know for sure that AI self-driving cars will overtake the conventional car, and so it is just conjecture or speculation. That being said, the marketplace sure believes that AI self-driving cars are going to win out in this car evolution battle, and any auto maker that doesn't seem to express the same is going to suffer the wrath of the market. Right or wrong.

So, making cars is the presumed knitting of the auto makers. AI self-driving cars sure seem to be the next evolution of cars. As the famous line suggests, auto makers should stick to their knitting, meaning the making of cars, and presumably become makers of AI self-driving cars.

But, a self-driving car is not just a car, it's a car that is combined with AI. Some question whether the auto makers can really grasp the nature of AI and figure out how to deploy it into cars. Maybe some auto makers are not cut out to do AI self-driving cars. They are so shaped around and preoccupied by conventional cars that their ability to re-focus and re-shape to make AI self-driving cars is beyond their means.

This is why we've seen tech firms step into the AI self-driving car realm. If you believe that the AI part of the self-driving car equation is the crucial element, you might suggest that the tech firms have a better grasp of the AI and so they are sticking to their knitting, namely, the development of AI. There is some amount of market pressure on tech firms to do something about AI self-driving cars, in the sense that if AI self-driving cars are going to happen and become widespread, any tech firm that wasn't involved might be left outside the bonanza of tech aspects that will be integral to the AI self-driving car.

Thus, we seem to have two knittings happening at the same time. There's the knitting of making cars. There's the knitting of making AI. Which of those is the more important part of the AI self-driving car puzzle.

Car- Makers Must Push Toward AI Self-Driving Cars

By far, the pressure is more so on the car makers about pushing toward AI self-driving cars. Google's Waymo for example is not under the same kind of pressures as a pure auto maker. The marketplace perceives that Waymo is doing something cool and innovative, and that it might lead to something, but even if it doesn't get us to AI self-driving cars there is still lots of spin-off aspects to having pursued AI self-driving cars. And, the allure of Google's effort of AI self-driving cars attracts other hot high-tech talent to Google overall, merely because the AI self-driving cars reflects the kind of futuristic innovation that such high-tech talent cherishes overall, irrespective per se of the need for or success of the self-driving cars side of things.

For the auto makers, the marketplace perceives that any auto maker not whole hog into AI self-driving cars is on its own death march. Their basic survival is depending upon AI self-driving cars. The pressures are enormous on the auto makers. As we've seen, some of the auto makers are trying to go after AI self-driving cars on their own, some are partnering with high-tech firms, some are buying up high-tech firms, some are working in an auto maker consortium, and so on. One way or another, they each are finding a means to get engaged in pursuing AI self-driving cars.

They have to do so.

Not solely because of the future possibilities, but also because of the perceptions of today about whether they are a progressive firm or stuck in the mud. Whether they are horse and carriage minded by solely doing conventional cars, or whether they are space age minded and embracing AI self-driving cars. Today's market reacts to the signals sent by the auto makers as to where they sit on the spectrum of belief about AI self-driving cars.

In recap, auto makers are forced into the AI self-driving car momentum by the nature of their core business, and by what their competition is doing, and by what the market expects them to be doing. High-tech firms such as Google and Apple have the "luxury" of choosing to aim toward AI self-driving cars because it gets them reputational advantages, it attracts top tech talent, it showcases they are leading edge tech makers, and demonstrates their boldness and innovation. Oh, and it could be that down the road, someday, AI self-driving cars become prevalent and those high-tech firms might miss out since they weren't there from day one — that's kind of an aside, though, and not considered a make-or-break as it is with the auto makers.

At the Cybernetic AI Self-Driving Car Institute, we are developing AI software for self-driving cars.

Our motivation is similar to the high-tech firms in that we like the challenge of it, it has great benefits to society, it could save lives, it has tremendous potential for new tech spin-offs, and it could be a monetary bonanza, based on the predictions that the self-driving car market will be around $20 billion by 2024, $800 billion by 2035, and perhaps $7 trillion by 2050. It's a big money opportunity, for sure.

Beyond the auto makers and the tech firms, there's someone else that also cares about the emergence of AI self-driving cars. Someone that can see the future as either being a boon for them due to the advent of AI self-driving cars or that could be the destruction of their business.

I'm talking about the ridesharing firms.

Why would ridesharing companies care about whether or not AI self-driving cars are going to arrive?

Let's take a look at the business model of ridesharing companies. They are essentially a dating service. There are those that are looking for a date and those that are wanting to be a date.

You want to get a ride from the office over to the baseball field (you are seeking a date, one might say). You go into a mobile app and state your request. A human driver of a car sees your request and accepts it (these human drivers are looking for a date, one might say).

The human driver comes to you, you get into the car, the human driver drives you to the baseball field.

Assume for the moment that the human driver was not employed per se by the ridesharing service and merely was "connected" to you via the ridesharing service (the middle man, so to speak), and happened to be a human driver registered with the ridesharing service (acting in an independent contractor role). The ridesharing service takes a fee for having arranged for the date.

In order for the ridesharing service to be successful, it has to attract those seeking a date, i.e., those needing a ride. Success of attraction will predominantly be based on whether or not the ridesharing service can on a timely basis provide a suitable date, as in providing a human driver in a car that can as quickly as possible reach you and then suitably drive you to your destination.

Do you care that much about the ridesharing service provider per se? Not really. Many people have both Uber and Lyft apps on their smartphones, and they shop as to which one can provide the suitable ride to them. We can quibble about the pricing as to whether there is a difference, and we can quibble about whether the drivers or their cars are better or worse, but by-and-large most would generally agree that there isn't any significant difference between picking one of the other.

How will AI self-driving cars impact these ridesharing services?

Remove the human driver from the equation. Instead, imagine that there are self-driving cars. Furthermore, these self-driving cars can be owned by just about anybody. You personally decide to buy an AI self-driving car, and while at work during the day, you are willing to have your AI self-driving car driving around for ridesharing purposes. You do this to make some extra bucks off of your AI self-driving car.

Today's ridesharing services need to attract human drivers with cars so as to provide a ready service to the ride seekers. With the advent of AI self-driving cars, ridesharing services will need to attract AI self-driving cars to be a ready service for ride seekers. Where will the ridesharing services find these AI self-driving cars?

Options for Ridesharing Services to Incorporate AI Self-Driving Cars

One approach would be for the ridesharing service to purchase AI self-driving cars and use them as a fleet. This could work, but it is big change for the ridesharing services since they would need to own these assets and presumably take care of them, including the maintenance and upkeep of the AI self-driving cars. That's not what they do today. They don't own any of the cars. They are a match making service.

Also, even if they decided to get into the car ownership for AI self-driving cars, it would be hard to predict how many such AI self-driving cars to have. Could they have so many that they could sufficiently meet demand? And, it would also be quite hard to predict where best to position geographically the AI self-driving cars for use. No, I don't think we'll likely see the ridesharing services opt to buy AI self-driving cars in huge bulk quantities and try to deploy them.

So, what else can they do?

They can appeal to the owners of the AI self-driving cars. Make money off your AI self-driving car by listing it with the XYZ ridesharing service. The ridesharing services make the same kind of plea today to human drivers. But, there's a big difference in the future because they are now making the plea to the owners of the AI self-driving cars. The owner isn't a driver. The AI is the driver.

Why should these owners of AI self-driving cars decide that they will list their vehicle with the XYZ ridesharing service? Maybe they would list their AI self-driving car with many ridesharing services, figuring it increases the odds of their AI self-driving car being kept in-use. Ridesharing services would likely fiercely compete with each other to try to prevent this, offering deals for exclusivity, and seek to have the owner dedicate their AI self-driving car to just one ridesharing service, but doing so will be tricky to achieve (and some say darned near impossible).

It gets worse though for the ridesharing services. Since this is really a match making service, the larger the pool of potential dates, the better it tends to be for those seeking a date and those offering to be a date. In that case, presumably any large-scale social media venue could do the same thing.

Estimates are that Uber for example has around 75 million users of its app, and Uber has perhaps 3 million or so registered drivers. Those seem like big numbers. But, let's consider the size of Facebook, which has around 2.2 billion users. That dwarfs the Uber numbers. If those Facebook users opted to list their AI self-driving cars for use, imagine the reach it would provide. All that Facebook would need to do is provide a software feature enabling the "dating" aspects, which isn't that hard to do.

And, there's a another twist to the ridesharing future too. Suppose that blockchain becomes popular and as such we might not have any "middle man" per se involved in ridesharing services aspects. Instead, on a purely P2P basis, we would jointly use a specialized blockchain floating on the Internet to which we could make our own matches for ridesharing purposes. I would post my AI self-driving car as to its availability along with millions of others that own AI self-driving cars. Ride seekers would merely inspect the blockchain to find a suitable ride. Prices and other details might perhaps be auto-negotiated or already stated via the blockchain. Etc. This though has some holes to it in terms of the reality of making it work, and so let's mark this as somewhat speculative for now.

Uber and Lyft have mainly today as their secret sauce that they are able to connect you with a human driver that has a car and that is a form of matching making to provide as a ridesharing capability.

Today's ridesharing services realize they are in a race against time. The sooner that AI self-driving cars emerge, the sooner they begin to lose out of their existing core business. The sooner too it becomes possible for other social media to overtake their business.

You might say that the ridesharing services should somehow try to impede the emergence of AI self-driving cars, trying desperately to stave off what seems like a sour future for them. But, it makes no sense to suggest that ridesharing services could somehow prevent or inhibit the progress toward AI self-driving cars. How would they do this? Maybe try to push regulators to enact tougher laws on AI self-driving cars and thus curtail the public road trials? Insist that human drivers are much safer than true AI self-driving cars? Or take some other such means.

As another famous line suggests, if you can't beat them, join them. That's what some of the ridesharing services have decided. Maybe they ought to get into the game and be a maker of AI self-driving cars. This seems somewhat logical not only because of the fact they are already in the business of cars, somewhat, but also because they are really a high-tech firm more than anything else. When you consider it for a moment, you realize that an Uber or Lyft is mainly a mobile app developer along with the back-end systems to support it. They developed a system that allows for what some call frictionless ridesharing.

Are the ridesharing services AI firms? Generally, no. That's why they have tended to buy their way into the AI space. Or, more specifically the AI self-driving car space.

What does this gain a ridesharing firm? If they can be the first to achieve AI self-driving cars, it can provide several potential advantages. It can establish them as the way in which you should be booking your ridesharing and maybe that would increase their base of ride seekers. It could attract more ride seekers that are enamored of the allure of being driven in an AI self-driving car. It could allow them to possibly lock-down the underlying technology and the Intellectual Property (IP), perhaps preventing others from deploying AI self-driving cars, or maybe becoming a huge licensing and money maker for them to others that want to also provide AI self-driving cars. Etc.

Now that I've laid the groundwork for examining the landscape of the major players consisting of auto makers, tech firms, and ridesharing firms as it relates to developing AI self-driving cars, let's take a closer look at Uber as an example of the troubling times afoot regarding AI self-driving cars for a ridesharing firm.

You likely know that Dara Khosrowshahi became the CEO of Uber about a year ago. The AI self-driving car unit of Uber has been steadily losing money, which generally is quite logical because it is primarily an R&D element. Putting company resources into R&D is always a hedge bet. You are betting that the money spent will ultimately achieve a return, but it could be quite a while before you can convert that R&D into something that can earn a return.

It was reported in the New York Times that upon Dara's first coming on-board that he had doubts about whether to continue to pour money into the AI self-driving car side of things (which is estimated losing them perhaps $100-$200 million per quarter). Apparently, once he had a chance to see it in action, he was swayed toward keeping it going. But, after the Uber incident in Arizona that led to the killing of a pedestrian, allegedly he swayed back over to being less committed to the venture.

This seesawing of desire to keep the unit "as is" versus considering some other alternatives makes business sense when you consider the ramifications of the unit and the conundrum involved.

Let's first consider the downsides.

It is unlikely that the unit will be a money maker any time soon.

Furthermore, it holds the peril of tarnishing the overall Uber brand due to any additional complications or incidents that might arise when doing the public trials of their AI self-driving cars. Deaths and injuries make the news, especially as it relates to AI self-driving cars. Potential public backlash to such incidents and the prospects of heavy regulatory oversight looms as a huge hammer that could harm the company in a multitude of ways.

Uber is also trying to get itself primed for an IPO. Firms usually tidy up and want to look as pretty as they can be to then make a big splash when going public. Having the AI self-driving car unit would maybe add brownie points to market perceptions, since it suggests a path to the future and showcases Uber's innovation and boldness. But, if the unit suffers any ill-timed hiccups leading up to the IPO, imagine the devastating impact it could have on the IPO. If by bad luck they had an AI self-driving car crash and injury/death just days before the IPO, they'd be in a rather sticky situation of whether to proceed or not (and, if they did proceed, it could undermine the opening price and perceived value of the firm).

Some might say that the tail has the potential to wag the dog.

Right now, the presumed market focus should be on their existing ridesharing service and not be distracted by the future possibilities involving AI self-driving cars.

Some say that they should just close down their AI self-driving car ambitions. But, if they suddenly opted to shut down the AI self-driving car unit due to the concerns that some malady might happen leading up to the IPO, or due to its present money-draining aspects, it would be a shocker to the market and have equally undesirable reactions. The unit is already on the radar of the marketplace. There would also be questions raised about the investments made to-date and why there isn't some means to presumably recoup it. And so on.

Some suggest that they could try to sell it. This would potentially provide an influx of monies and help the firm from a financial posture going into the IPO. If they sold it outright, it might though lead to questions about what is their intended future for AI self-driving cars. It could leave a gap or unanswered question. In that sense, it could be that it might make sense to undertake a sale that was coupled with some arrangements for Uber to have an ongoing stake, or maybe Uber barters a licensing deal to use the AI self-driving cars once perfected, or similar kind of arrangements might be made.

It is important to realize too that AI self-driving cars won't magically overnight become prevalent. I've predicted many times that there will be an ongoing mixture of conventional cars and AI self-driving cars for years to come. In the United States alone, there are 200+ million conventional cars, and they aren't going to suddenly disappear and nor will they immediately be converted over to AI self-driving cars (if such a conversion or "kit" approach is even viable).

Thus, in theory, ridesharing services will continue with their present model for quite some time to come, meaning that they will still be seeking human drivers of conventional cars, and then later on human drivers of AI self-driving cars that are not true AI self-driving cars. Gradually, the ridesharing services would include true AI self-driving cars. The mix of proportions of their ridesharing offerings would consist primarily now of the human driven approaches and only a minor amount of true AI self-driving cars, and the mix would over time slowly shift in the other direction.

For ridesharing services, it is the best of times, it is the worst of times. Ridesharing has shifted from being a novelty to becoming a new cornerstone of travel. Currently, ridesharing is riding the wave. Making money off of ridesharing is still a challenge and it is a bit of optimistic faith to believe that it will be a tremendous money maker as the future unfolds. Up ahead looms the advent of AI self-driving cars. Ridesharing firms can't ignore what's coming down the pike. The question arises as to what is their best strategy right now regarding AI self-driving cars, and the degree to which they must either be invested in AI self-driving cars directly versus being merely affiliated with AI self-driving cars. Stay tuned.

CHAPTER 10

MULTI-PARTY PRIVACY
AND
AI SELF-DRIVING CARS

CHAPTER 10

MULTI-PARTY PRIVACY
AND
AI SELF-DRIVING CARS

You are at a bar and a friend of yours takes a selfie that includes you in the picture. Turns out you've had a bit to drink and it's not the most flattering of pictures. In fact, you look totally plastered. You are so hammered that you don't even realize that your friend is taking the selfie and the next morning you don't even remember there was a snapshot taken of the night's efforts. About three days later, after becoming fully sober, you happen to look at the social media posts of your friend, and lo-and-behold there's the picture, posted for her friends to see.

In a semi-panic, you contact your friend and plead with the friend to remove the picture. The friend agrees to do so. Meanwhile, turns out that the friends of that person happened to capture the picture, and many of them thought it was so funny that they re-posted it in other venues. It's now on Facebook, Instagram, Twitter, etc. You look so ridiculous that it has gone viral. Some have even cutout just you from the picture and then made memes of you that are hilarious, and have spread like wildfire on social media.

People at work that only know you at work (you don't often associate with them outside of the workplace), have come up to you at the office to mention they saw the picture. Your boss comes to ask you about it. The company is a bit worried that it might somehow reflect poorly on the firm.

People that you used to know from high school and even elementary school have contacted you to say that you've really gone wild (you used to be the studious serious person). Oddly enough, you know that this was a one-time drinking binge and that you almost never do anything like this. You certainly hadn't been anticipating that a picture would capture the rare moment. Frustratingly, it's a complete mischaracterization of who you are. A momentary lapse that has been blown way out of proportion.

People that you don't know start to bombard your social media sites with requests to get linked. Anyone that parties that hard must be worth knowing. Unfortunately, most of the requests are from creepy people. Scarier still is that they have Googled you and found out all sorts of aspects about your personal life. These complete strangers are sending you messages that appear as though they know you, doing so by referring to places you've lived, vacations you've taken, and so on.

Sadly, this leads to identity theft attempts of your identity, such as your bank account or opening of credit cards, and so on. It leads to cyberstalking of you by nefarious hackers. Social phishing ensues.

If this seems like a nightmare, I'd say that you can wake-up now and go along with the aspect that it was all a dream. A really ugly dream.

Let's also make clear that it could absolutely happen.

Many people that are using social media seem to not realize that their privacy is not necessarily controlled solely by themselves. If you end-up in someone else's snapshot that just so happens to include you, maybe you are in the tangentially foreground or maybe even in the background, there's a chance that you'll now be found on social media if that person posts the photo.

The advent of facial recognition for photos has become quite proficient. In the early days of social media, a person's face had to be facing completely forward and fully seen by the camera, the lighting had to be topnotch, and basically if it was a pristine kind of facial shot then the computer could recognize your face. Also, there were so few faces on social media that the computer could only determine that there was a face present, but it wasn't able to try and guess who's face it was.

Nowadays, the facial recognition is so good that your head can be turned and barely seen by the camera, and the lighting can be crummy, and there can be blurs and other aspects, and yet the computer can find a face. And, it can label the face by using the now millions of faces already found and tagged. The odds of remaining in obscurity in a photo online is no longer feasible for very long.

People are shocked to find that they went to the mall and all of a sudden there's some postings that have them tagged in the photos. You are likely upset because you were just minding your own business at the mall. You didn't take a photo of yourself and nor did a friend. But, because other people were taking photos, and because of the widespread database of faces, once these fellow mall shoppers posted the picture, it was easy enough to automatically tag you in the photo by a computer. No human intervention needed.

Notice also that in the story about being in a bar and a friend having taken a snapshot, even if your friend agrees to remove the picture from being posted, the odds are that once it's been posted you'll never be able to stop it from being promulgated. There's a rule-of-thumb these days that once something gets posted, it could be that it will last forever (unless you believe that someday the Internet will be closed down – good luck waiting for that day).

I realize you are likely already thinking about your own privacy when it comes to your own efforts, such as a selfie of yourself that you made and that you posted. You might be very diligent about only posting selfies that you think showcase your better side. You might be careful to not post a blog that might use foul words or offend anyone. You might be cautious about filling in forms at web sites and be protective about private information.

Unfortunately, unless you live on a deserted island, the odds are that you are around other people, and the odds are that those people are going to capture you in their photos. I suppose you could walk around all day long with a bag over your head. When people ask you why, you could tell them you are trying to preserve your privacy. You are trying to remain anonymous. I'd bet that you'd get a lot of strange stares and possibly people calling the police to come check-out the person wearing the bag over their head.

In some cases, you'll perhaps know that you are in a photo and that someone that you know is going to post it. You went to a friend's birthday party on Saturday and photos were taken. The friend already mentioned that an online photo album had been setup. You'll be appearing in those photos. That's something you knew about beforehand. There's also the circumstance of being caught up in a photo that you didn't know was being taken, and might have been a snapshot by a complete stranger, akin to the mall example earlier.

So, let's recap:

- You took a selfie, which you knew about because you snapped it, and then you posted it

- You end-up in someone else's photo, whom you know, and they posted it, but you didn't know they would post it

- You end-up in someone else's photo, whom you know, and they posted it with your blessings

- You end-up in someone else's photo, a complete stranger, and they posted it but you didn't know they would post it

- You took a photo of others, whom you know, and you posted it, but you didn't let them know beforehand

- You took a photo of others, whom you know, and you posted it with their blessings

- You took a photo of others, complete strangers, and you posted it but they didn't know you would post it

- Etc.

I purposely have pointed out in the aforementioned list that you can be both the person "victimized" by this and also the person that causes others to be victimized. I say this because I know some people that have gotten upset that others included them in a photo, and posted it without getting the permission of that person, and yet this same person routinely posts photos that include others and they don't get their permission. Do as I say, not as I do, that's the mantra of those people.

There's a phrase for this multitude of participants involved in privacy, namely it is referred to as Multi-Party Privacy (MP).

Multi-Party Privacy has to do with trying to figure out what to do about intersecting privacy aspects in a contemporary world of global social media.

You might be thinking that privacy is a newer topic and that it has only emerged with the rise of the Internet and social media. Well, you might be surprised then to know that in 1948 the United Nations adopted a document known as the Universal Declaration of Human Rights (UDHR) and Article 12 refers to the right of privacy. Of course, few at that time could envision fully the world we have today, consisting of a globally interconnected electronic communications network and the use of social media, and for which it has made trying to retain or control privacy a lot harder to do.

When you have a situation involving MP, you can likely have an issue arise with conflict among the participants in terms of the nature of the privacy involved. In some cases, there is little or no conflict and the MP might be readily dealt with, thus it is easy to ensure the privacy of the multiple participants. More than likely, you'll have to deal with Multi-Party Privacy Conflicts (MPC), wherein one or more parties disagree about the privacy aspects of something that intersects them.

In the story about you being in the bar and your friend snapped the unbecoming picture and posted it, you might have been perfectly fine with this and therefore there was no MPC. But, as per the story, you later on realized what had happened, and so you objected to your friend about the posting. This was then a conflict.

This was a MPC: Multi-parties involved in a matter of privacy, over which they have a conflict, because one of them was willing to violate the privacy of the other, but the other was not willing to do so.

In this example, your friend quickly acquiesced and agreed to remove the posting. This seemingly resolved the MPC.

As mentioned, even if the MPC seems to be resolved, it can unfortunately be a situation wherein the horse is already out of the barn. The damage is done and cannot readily be undone. Privacy can be usurped, even if the originating point of the privacy breech is later somehow fixed or undone.

I realize that some of you will say that you've had such a circumstance and that rather than trying to un-post the picture that you merely removed the tag that had labeled you in the picture. Yes, many of the social media sites allow you to un-tag something that was either manually tagged or automatically tagged. This would seem to then put you back into anonymity.

If so, it is likely short-lived. All it will take is for someone else to come along and decide to re-apply a tag, or an automated crawler that does it. Trying to return to a state of anonymity is going to be very hard to do as long as the picture still remains available. There will always be an open chance that it will get tagged again.

I'll scare you even more so. There are maybe thousands of photos right now with you in them, perhaps in the background while at the train station, or while in a store, or at a mall, or on vacation in the wilderness. You might not yet be tagged in any of those. The more that we continue to move toward this global massive inter-combining of social media and the Internet, and the more that computers advance and computing power becomes less costly, those seemingly "obscure" photos are bound to get labeled.

Every place that you've ever been, in every photo so captured, and that's posted online, might ultimately become a tagged indication of where you were. Plus, the odds are that the photo has embedded in it other info such as the date and time of the photo, and the latitude and longitude of the photo location. Not only are you tagged, but now we'll know when you were there and where it was. Plus, whomever else is in the photo will be tagged, so we'll all know who you were with.

Yikes! Time to give it all up, and go live in a cave. Say, are there any cameras in that cave?

What does all this have to do with AI self-driving cars?

At the Cybernetic AI Self-Driving Car Institute, we are developing AI software for self-driving cars.

We're also aware of the potential privacy aspects and looking at ways to deal with them from a technology perspective (it will also need to be dealt with from a societal and governmental perspective too).

I've also pointed out that many of the pundits in support of AI self-driving cars continually hammer away at the benefits of AI self-driving cars, such as the mobility possibilities, but they often do so with idealism and don't seem to be willing to also consider the downsides such as privacy concerns.

Some are worried that we're heading towards a monstrous future by having AI self-driving cars, including the potential for large-scale privacy invasion, as such, including considering an AI self-driving car as a Frankenstein moment.

Herein, let's take a close look at Multi-Party Privacy and the potential for conflicts, or MPC as it relates to AI self-driving cars.

An AI self-driving car involves these key aspects as part of the driving task:
- Sensor data collection and interpretation
- Sensor fusion
- Virtual world model updating
- AI action plans
- Car controls commands issuance

This is based on my overarching framework about AI self-driving cars (see Chapter 1).

You would normally think about the sensors of an AI self-driving car that are facing outward and detecting the world around the self-driving car. There are cameras involved, radar, sonar, LIDAR, and the like. These are continually scanning the surroundings and allow the AI to then ascertain as best feasible whether there is a car ahead, or whether there might be a pedestrian nearby, and so on. Sometimes one kind of sensor might be blurry or not getting a good reading, and thus the other sensors are more so relied upon. Sometimes they are all working well and a generally full sensing of the environment will be possible.

One question for you is how long will this collected data about the surroundings be kept? You could argue that the AI only needs the collected data from moment to moment. You are driving down a street in a neighborhood. As you proceed along, every second the sensors are collecting data. The AI is reviewing it to ascertain what's going on. You might assume that this is a form of data streaming and there's no "collection" per se of it.

You'd likely be wrong in that assumption. Some or all of that data might indeed be collected and retained. For the on-board systems of the self-driving car, perhaps only portions are being kept. The AI self-driving car likely has an OTA (Over The Air) updating capability, allowing it to use some kind of Internet-like communications to connect with an in-the-cloud capability of the auto maker or tech firm that made the AI system. The data being collected by the AI self-driving car can potentially be beamed to the cloud via the OTA.

There are some AI developers that are going to be screaming right now and saying that Lance, there's no way that the entire set of collected data from each AI self-driving car is going to be beamed-up. It's too much data, it takes too much time to beam-up. And, besides, it's wasted effort because what would someone do with the data? I'd counter-argue that with compression and with increasingly high-speed communications, it's not so infeasible to beam-up the data. Plus, the data could be stored temporarily on-board the self-driving car and then piped up at a later time.

In terms of what the data could be used for, well, that's the million-dollar question. Or, maybe billion-dollar question.

If you were an auto maker or tech firm, and you could collect the sensory data from the AI self-driving cars that people have purchased from you, would you want to do so? Sure, why not. You could use it presumably to improve the capabilities of the AI self-driving cars, mining the data and improving the machine learning capabilities across all of your AI self-driving cars. That's a pretty clean and prudent thing to do.

You could also use the data in case there are accidents involving your AI self-driving car. By examining the data after an accident, perhaps you'd be able show that the dog that the AI self-driving car hit was hidden from view and darted out into the street at the last moment. This might be crucial from a public perception that the seemingly evil AI ran over a dog in the roadway. The data might also have important legal value. It might be used for lawsuits against the auto maker or tech firm. It might be used for insurance purposes to set rates of insurance. Etc.

Let's also though put on our money making hats. If you were an auto maker or tech firm, and you were collecting all of this data, could you make money from it? Would third parties be willing to pay for that data? Maybe so. When you consider that the AI self-driving car is driving around all over the place, and it is kind of mapping whatever it encounters, there's bound to be business value in that data.

It could have value to the government too. Suppose your AI self-driving car was driving past a gas station just as a thief ran out of the attached convenience store. Voila, your AI self-driving car might have captured the thief on the video that was being used by the AI to navigate the self-driving car.

In essence, with the advent of AI self-driving cars, wherever we are, whenever we are there, the roaming AI self-driving cars are now going to up the ante on video capture. If you already were leery about the number of video cameras that are on rooftops and walls and polls, the AI self-driving car is going to increase that exponentially.

Don't think of the AI self-driving car as a car, instead think of it as a roaming video camera. Right now, there are 200+ million cars in the United States. Imagine if every of those cars had a video camera, and the video camera had to be on whenever the car was in motion. That's a lot of video. That's a lot of video of everyday activities.

I challenge you to later today, when in your car, look around and pretend that all the other cars have video cameras and are recording everything they see, every moment. Eerie, yes?

The point herein that if you believe in the Multi-Party Privacy issue, the AI self-driving car is going to make the MP become really big-time. And, the MPC, the conflicts over privacy, will go through the roof.

You opt to take your AI self-driving car to the local store. It captures video of your neighbors outside their homes, mowing the lawn, playing ball with their kids, watching birds, you name it. All of that video, in the normal everyday course of life activities. Suppose it gets posted someplace online. Did any of them agree to this? Would then even know they had been recorded?

I assure you that the sensors and video cameras on an AI self-driving car are so subtle that people are not going to realize that they are being recorded. It's not like the old days where there might be a large camera placed on the top of the car and someone holding up a sign saying you are being recorded. It will be done without any realization by people. Even if at first they are thinking about it, once AI self-driving cars become prevalent it will just become an accustomed aspect. And, suppose the government mandated that a red recording light had to be placed on the top of an AI self-driving car, what would people do? Stop playing ball in the street, hide behind a tree, or maybe walk around all day with a bag over their heads? Doubtful.

One unanswered question right now is whether you as the owner of an AI self-driving car will get access to the sensor data collected by your AI self-driving car. You might insist that of course you should, it's your car, darn it. The auto makers and tech firms might disagree and say that the data collected is not your data, it is data owned by them. They can claim you have no right to it, and furthermore that you're having it might undermine the privacy of others. We'll need to see how that plays out in real life.

Let's also consider the sensors that will be pointing inward into the AI self-driving car. Yes, I said pointing inward.

There is likely to be both audio microphones inside the AI self-driving car and cameras pointing inward. Why? Suppose you put your children into the AI self-driving car and tell the AI to take them to school. I'm betting you'd want to be able to see your children and make sure they are Okay. You'd want to talk to them and let them talk to you. For this a myriad of other good reasons, there's going to be cameras and microphones inwardly aimed inside AI self-driving cars.

If you were contemplating the privacy aspects of recording what the AI self-driving car detects outside of the self-driving car, I'm sure you'll be dismayed at the recordings of what's happening inside the AI self-driving car.

Here's an example. It's late at night. You've been to the bar. You want to get home. You are at least aware enough to not drive yourself. You hail an AI self-driving car. You get into the AI self-driving car, there's no human driver. While in the AI self-driving car, you hurl whatever food and drink you had ingested while at the bar. You freak out inside the AI self-driving car due to the drunkenness and you ramble about how bad your life is. You yell about the friends that don't love you. You are out of your head.

Suppose the AI self-driving car is a ridesharing service provided by the Acme company. They now have recorded all of your actions while inside the AI self-driving car. What might they do with it? There's also the chance that the ridesharing service is actually somebodies personal AI self-driving car, but they let it be used when they aren't using it, trying to earn some extra dough. They now have that recording of you in the AI self-driving car.

Eerie, yes?

There might be some AI self-driving ridesharing services that advertise they will never ever violate your privacy and that they don't record what happens inside their AI self-driving cars.

Or, there might be AI ridesharing services that offer for an extra fee they won't record. Or, for an extra fee they will give you a copy of the recording.

You might say that it is a violation of your privacy to have such a recording made. But, keep in mind that you willingly went into the AI self-driving car. There might even be some kind of agreement you agreed to by booking the ridesharing service or by getting into the self-driving car.

Some have suggested that once people know they are being recorded inside of a self-driving car, they'll change their behavior and behave. This seems so laughable that I can barely believe the persons saying this believe it. Maybe when AI self-driving cars first begin, we'll sit in them like we used to do in an airplane, and be well-mannered and such, but after AI self-driving cars become prevalent, human behavior will be human behavior.

There are some that are exploring ways to tackle this problem using technology. Perhaps, when you get into the AI self-driving car, you have some kind of special app on your smartphone that can mask the video being recorded by the self-driving car and your face is not shown and your voice is scrambled. Or, maybe there is a bag in the self-driving car that you can put over your head (oops, back to the bag trick).

The Multi-Party Privacy issue arises in this case because there is someone else potentially capturing your private moments and it is in conflict with how you want your private moments to be used. Let's extend this idea. You get into an AI self-driving car with two of your friends. You have a great time in the self-driving car. Afterward, one of you wants to keep and post the video, the other does not. There's another MPC.

Some people will like having the video recordings of the interior of the AI self-driving car. Suppose you take the family on a road trip. You might want to keep the video of both the interior shenanigans and the video captured of where you went. In the past, you might show someone a few pictures of your family road trip. Nowadays, you tend to show them video clips. In the future, you could show the whole trip, at least from the perspective of whatever the AI self-driving car could see.

I hope that this discussion about Multi-Party Privacy does not cause you to become soured on AI self-driving cars. Nor do I want this to be something of an alarmist nature. The point more so is that we need to be thinking now about what the future will consist of. The AI developers crafting AI self-driving cars are primarily focused on getting an AI self-driving car to be able to drive. We need to be looking further ahead, and considering what other qualms or issues might arise. I'd bet that MPC will be one of them. Get ready for privacy conflicts. There are going to be conflicts about conflicts, you betcha.

Lance B. Eliot

CHAPTER 11

CHAFF BUGS AND
AI SELF-DRIVING CARS

CHAPTER 11

CHAFF BUGS AND AI SELF-DRIVING CARS

In the movie remake of the Thomas Crown Affair, the main character opts to go into an art museum to ostensibly steal a famous work of art, and does so attired in the manner of The Son of Man artwork (a man wearing a bowler hat and an overcoat). Spoiler alert, he arranges for dozens of other men to come into the museum dressed similarly as he, thus confounding the efforts by the waiting police that had been tipped that he would come there to commit his thievery. By having many men serving as decoys, he pulls off the effort and the police are exasperated at having to check the numerous decoys and yet are unable to nab him (he sneakily changes his clothes).

This ploy was a clever use of deception.

During World War II, there was the invention of chaff, which was also a form of deception. Radar had just emerged as a means to detect flying airplanes and therefore be able to try and more accurately shoot them down. The radar device would send a signal that would bounce off the airplane and provide a return to the radar device, thus allowing detection of where the airplane was. It was hypothesized that there might be a means to confuse the radar device by putting something into the air that would seem like an airplane but was not an airplane. At first, the idea was to have something suspended from an airplane or maybe have balloons or parachutes that could contain a material that would bounce back the radar signals.

A flying airplane could potentially release the parachutes or balloons that had the radar reflecting material. After exploring this notion, it was further advanced by the discovery that pieces of metal foil could be dropped from the airplane and that it was be an easier way to create this deception. The first versions were envisioned as acting in a double-duty fashion, doing so by being the size of a sheet of paper and contain propaganda written on them. This would be providing a twofer (two-for-one), it would confuse the radar and then once landed on the ground it would serve as a propaganda leaflet.

Turns out that the use of strips of aluminum foil were much more effective. This nixed the propaganda element of the idea. With the strips, you could dump out hundreds or even thousands of the strips all at once, bundled together but intended to float apart from each other once made airborne. These strips will flutter around and the radar would ping off of them. With a cloud of them floating in the air, the radar would be overwhelmed and unable to identify where the airplane was.

Interestingly, this was considered such a significant defensive weapon that neither the Allies and nor the Germans were willing to use them after they had each independently discovered the invention. It was thought that once used, even if used just one time, the other side would then also discover it and be able to use the same.

We have two examples then of the use of decoys for deception purposes. One is the bowler hat attired character in a movie, the other is the real-world use during World War II. Of course, there are many other ways in life that you might come across these kinds of ploys. One such relatively newer such use applies to computer software.

Researchers at NYU had recently posted a paper about their use of chaff bugs in software (work done by Zhenghao Hu, Yu Hu, and Brendan Dolan-Gavitt). This reuse of the old "decoys trickery" is an intriguing modern approach to trying to bolster computer security. Some of you will find it curious. Some of you will think it genius. Some of you with think it silly and unworkable.

Here's the deal.

We already know that computer hackers (in this case, the word "hackers" is being used to imply thieves or hooligans) will often try to find some exploitable aspect of a software program so that they can then get the program to do something to their bidding or otherwise act in an untoward manner. Famous exploits include being able to force a buffer overflow, which then might allow the program to suddenly get access to areas of memory it normally should not. Or, it might be that the exploit causes the program to come to a halt or crash. This might be desirable by the hacker either to allow them to take some other action because perhaps the program was acting as a guardian, or that it might cause havoc or confusion that the hacker is hoping to stoke.

Indeed, in the recent news, there was a reveal that certain HP All-in-One printers could be sent a rigged image to the fax machine portion of the printer, and it would cause a buffer overflow that then could allow for someone remotely to get the printer to engage in its built-in remote code execution mode. Once in the remote code execution mode, the nefarious person could get the printer to do other potentially bad things by sending it additional code and commands. Plus, if the printer was behind a firewall and had internal network access, you could possibly sneak into other of the network connected devices too.

Skilled such hackers are continually on the look for exploits in software. These are usually small clips of code that can be turned into aiding the evil doing of the hacker. Generally, this is high skilled work to find the exploits and then devise a means to leverage the exploit. I say that because most of the time when you hear in the news about some "hacker" that got into a person's computer or email, it is something very low-tech such as they guessed that the person used a password like "12345" and the "hacker" simply used that to break-in.

By the way, these simpleton kinds of break-in's of guessing passwords are somewhat demeaning to the highly skilled hackers. If you are hunter that is trained and has years of experience in how to use a gun and hunt for wild boar, you are pretty irked when someone at a campground puts out some strips of bacon and the wild boar lands in their lap. Irked because those that don't know about hunting will equate the trained and experienced hunter with the idiot that happened to have the bacon.

In any case, when developing software, well-versed software engineers and programmers should be trying to avoid writing something that can become an exploit. If you have in-depth knowledge of the programming language you are using, you should already have familiarity with the known potential exploits that you can fall into. Unfortunately, not all programmers are versed in this, or they are so pressured to write the code quickly that they don't think about the potential for exploits, or they are not aware of how the code will be compiled and run such that maybe it creates an exploit that they would not otherwise have anticipated. And so on.

Let's get back to the researchers and what they came up with. They were trying to develop software that would find exploits in software. Indeed, there are various tools that you can use to find potential exploits. The hackers use these tools. Such tools can also be used by those that want to scan their own software and try to find exploits, hopefully doing so before they actually release their software. It would be handy to catch the exploits beforehand, rather than having them arise at a bad time, or allow someone nefarious to find them and use them.

To be able to properly test a tool that seeks to find exploits, you need to have a testbed of software that has potential exploits and thus you can run your detective tool on that testbed. Presumably, the tool should be able to find the exploits, which you know are in the testbed. This helps to then verify that the tool apparently works as hoped for. If the tool cannot find exploits that you know are embedded into the testbed, you'd need to take a closer look at the tool and try to figure out why it missed finding the exploit. This cycle is repeated over and over, until you believe that the tool is catching all of the exploits that you purposely seeded into the testbed.

So, you need to create a testbed that has a lot of potential exploits. It can be laborious to think of and write a ton of such exploits. You can find many of them online and copy them, but it is still a quite labor intensive process. Therefore, it would be handy to have a tool that would generate exploits or potential exploits which you could then insert into or "inject" into a software testbed.

With me so far?

Here's the final twist.

If you had a tool that could create potential exploits, doing so for purposes of creating test exploits to be put into a testbed of software, you could also consider potentially using the ability to generate potential exploits to create decoys for use in real software.

Think of each of the potential exploits as akin to a strip of foil for the World War II chaff. For the WWII chaff, you'd have lots and lots of the strips, so as to overwhelm the enemy radar. Why not do the same for software by generating say hundreds or maybe even thousands of potential exploits, clips of code, and then embed those clips of code into the software that you are otherwise developing.

This could then serve to trick any hacker that is aiming to look into your code. They would find tons of these potential exploits. Now, you'd of course want to make sure that these seeded exploits are non-exploitable. In other words, you'd be shooting your own foot if you were generating true exploits. You want instead ones that look like the real thing, but that are in fact not exploitable.

The hacker then would be faced with having to find a needle in a haystack, meaning that even if you have a real exploit in your code, presumably done unintentionally and you didn't catch it beforehand, the hacker now is faced with thousands of potential exploits and the odds of finding the true one is lessened. This would raise the barrier to entry, so to speak, in that the hacker now has to spend an inordinate amount of time and effort to possibly find the true exploit, even if it exists, which it might not.

I realize that the initial reaction is that it seems somewhat surprising, maybe ludicrous, for you to purposely put potential exploits into your code. Even if they are truly and utterly non-exploitable, it still just seems like you are playing with fire. When you play with fire, you can get burned. That's the concern for some, namely that if you inject your (hopefully) clean code with hundreds or thousands of potential non-exploitable exploits, it seems like something bad is bound to happen.

This might be similar to the famous line in the movie Ghostbusters when they were cautioned to not cross the streams of their ghostbuster energy guns, since it could cause an obliteration of the entire universe.

You could say that vaccines are dangerous and yet we use them on humans everyday. A vaccine is often a weakened version of the real underlying virus, and you use it to get the human body to react and build-up a defense. The defense then comes to play when a true wild attack of the virus occurs. This analogy though isn't quite apt for this matter since the non-exploitable exploits aren't bolstering the code of the software, instead they are there simply as decoys.

These so-called chaff bugs might be an effective kind of decoy. Would it scare off a hacker looking for exploits? Maybe yes, maybe no.

On the one hand, if the hacker looked at the overall code and found right away a potential exploit, they might get pretty excited and think it is their lucky day. They might then expend a lot of attention to the found exploit, which presumably if truly un-exploitable then is a waste of their time. Would they then give up, or would they look for another one? If they give up, great, the decoy did its thing. If they look for more, they'll certainly find more because we know that we've purposely put a bunch of them in there.

After finding numerous such potential exploits, and after discovering that they are non-exploitable, would then the hacker give up? This seems likely. It all depends too on how important it is to find a potential exploit. It also depends on how "good" the non-exploitable exploits are in terms of looking like a true exploit.

If the hacker can somehow readily figure out which are the injected exploits, they could then readily opt to ignore them. In that sense, we're back to the software essentially not having any of the decoys in it, in the sense that if the decoys are all readily discoverable, it's about the same as if you had none at all in your code.

Therefore, the decoys need to be "good" decoys in that they appear to be exploitable exploits and do not readily appear to be non-exploitable exploits. This can be tricky to achieve. Having an exploit that is non-exploitable can be achieved by doing some relatively simple things to mute or block the exploit's exploitability, but then it becomes very easy to look at the exploit and know that it is most likely a planted non-exploitable exploit.

In terms of the planting of the non-exploitable exploits, that's another factor to be considered. If I put the decoys in very obvious places of the code, the hacker might realize the underlying pattern of where I am putting the decoys. This then allows the hacker to either ignore those seeming exploits or at least realize that after some limited inspection that if it came from that area of the code it is more likely to be a planted one. You've got to then find a means to plant or inject the exploits so that their positioning in the code is not a giveaway.

You could consider randomly scattering the non-exploitable exploits throughout the software. This might not be so good. On the one hand, the randomness hopefully prevents a hacker from identifying a pattern to where the decoys were planted. At the same time, it could be that you've put an exploit in a part of the code that would not be advisable for it.

Allow me to explain.

If the non-exploitable exploits are to be convincing as potentially exploitable exploits, they presumably need to actually do something and cannot be just stubs of code that are blocked off from execution. A blocked off exploit would upon inspection be an obvious decoy and thus not require much further effort to explore. Remember that we want the presumed hacker to consume a lot of time by examining the decoys.

But, if the non-exploitable exploits are indeed able to execute then we need to be sure that not only don't they do something that a genuine exploit would do, we also need to be concerned about their execution time and the consumption of computing cycles. The decoy might be using up expensive computing cycles, doing so needlessly, other than to try and suggest that it is not a decoy. When I say expensive, I am referring to the notion that the computing cycles might be needed for other computational tasks, and so the decoy is robbing those tasks by chewing up cycles (in addition, you could say "expensive" depending upon what the cost is for your computing cycles).

The decoy might use up both computer cycles and also memory. Memory could also be a limited resource and therefore the decoy is using it up, solely for the purposes of trying to throw off a potential interloper. As such, however it is that the non-exploitable exploit works, it must appear to be a true exploit, and yet not do any harm, and also minimize consumption of precious computational cycles and computer memory. This is a bit of a tall order as to having non-exploitable exploits that can be such alluring decoys at the minimal overall cost possible.

We could opt to have let's say simple decoys and super decoys. The simple decoys are not very convincing and are readily detectable, while the super decoys are complex and difficult to detect as a decoy. Then, upon seeding of the source code, we might use a mixture of both the simple decoys and the super decoys. As mentioned before, though, it is important to refrain from putting any of the more time consuming or memory consuming decoys into areas of the code that might be especially adversely impacted. If there's a routine in the code that needs to run fast and tightly, putting a decoy into the middle of it would likely be unwise and detrimental.

What does this have to do with AI self-driving cars?

At the Cybernetic AI Self-Driving Car Institute, we are developing AI software for self-driving cars. As part of that effort, we are also exploring ways to try and protect the AI software, particularly once it is on-board a self-driving car and could potentially be hacked by someone with untoward intentions.

One approach to help make the AI software harder to figure out for an interloper involves making use of code obfuscation. This is a method in which you purposely make the source code difficult to logically comprehend.

Another possibility of a means to try and undermine an interloper would be to consider using chaff bugs in the AI software.

This has advantages and disadvantages. It has the potential to boost the security by a security-by-deception approach and might discourage hackers that are trying to delve into the system. A significant disadvantage would be whether the decoys would possibly undermine the system due to the real-time nature of the system. The AI needs to work under tight time constraints and must be making computational aspects that ultimately are controlling a moving car and for which the "decisions" made by the software are of a life-or-death nature. A decoy that placed in the wrong spot of the code and for which chews up on-board cycles could put the AI and humans at risk.

Consider that these are the major tasks of the AI for a self-driving car:

- Sensor data collection and interpretation

- Sensor fusion

- Virtual world model updating

- AI action plan updating

- Car controls command issuance

See my article about my framework for AI self-driving cars for more details about these tasks (see Chapter 1).

Where would it be "safe" to put the decoys? Safe in the sense that the execution of the decoy does not delay or interfere with the otherwise normal real-time operation of the system. It's dicey wherever you might be thinking to place the decoys.

We also need to consider the determination of the hacker.

If a hacker happens upon some software of any kind, they might be curious to try and hack it, and give up if they aren't sure whether the software itself does something of enough significance that it is worth their effort to continue trying to crack it. In the case of the AI software for a self-driving car, there is a lot of incentive to want to crack into the code, and so even if the decoys are present, and even if it becomes apparent to the hacker, and even if the hacker is somewhat discouraged, it would seem less likely they'd give up since the prize in the end has such high value.

Anyway, one of the members of our AI development team is taking a closer look at this potential use of chaff bugs. My view is that the team members are able to set aside a small percentage of their time toward innovation projects that might or might not lead to something of utility. It is becoming gradually somewhat popular as a technique among high-tech firms to allow their developers to have some "fun" time on projects of their own choosing. This boosts morale, gives them a break from their other duties, and might just land upon a goldmine.

One approach that we're exploring is whether Machine Learning (ML) can be used to aid in figuring out how to generate the non-exploitable exploits and also to make those decoys as realistically appearing to be integral to the code as we can get. By analyzing the style of the existing source code, the ML tries to take templates of non-exploitable exploits and see if they can be "personalized" as befits the source code. This would make those decoys even more convincing.

At an industry conference I mentioned the chaff bugs work, and I was asked about whether to hide them or whether to make them more obvious in some respects. The idea is that if you hide them well, the hacker might not realize they are faced with a situation of having to pore through purposely seeded non-exploitable exploits and so blindly just plow away and use up a lot of their effort needlessly.

On the other hand, if you make them more apparent, at least some of them, it might be a kind of warning to the hacker that they are faced with software that has gone to the trouble to make it very hard to find true exploits. You might consider this equivalent to putting a sign outside of your house that says the house is protected by burglar alarms. The sign alone might scare off a lot of potential intruders, even whether you have put in place the decoys or not (some people get a burglar alarm sign and put it on their house as merely a scare tactic).

For AI software that runs a self-driving car, I'd vote that we all ought to be making it as hard to crack into as we can. The auto makers and tech firms aren't putting as much attention to the security aspects as they perhaps should, since right now the AI self-driving cars are pretty much kept in their hands as they do testing and trial runs. Once true AI self-driving cars are being sold openly, the chances for the hackers to spend whatever amount of time they want to crack into the system goes up. We need to prepare for that eventually. If AI self-driving cars become prevalent, and yet they get hacked, it's going to be bad times for everyone, the auto makers, the tech firms, and the public at large. Chaff bugs and whatever other novel ideas arise, we're going to be taking a look and be kicking the tires to see if they'll be viable as a means to protect the AI systems of self-driving cars.

CHAPTER 12
SOCIAL RECIPROCITY
AND
AI SELF-DRIVING CARS

CHAPTER 12

SOCIAL RECIPROCITY
AND AI SELF-DRIVING CARS

Thank you for driving safely. Or, suppose instead I said to you that you should "Drive Safely: It's the Law" – how would you react? Perhaps I might say "Drive Safely or Get a Ticket." I could be even more succinct and simply say: Drive Safely.

These are all ways to generally say the same thing. Yet, how you react to them can differ quite a bit.

Why would you react differently to these messages that all seem to be saying the same thing? Because how the message is phrased will create a different kind of social context that your underlying social norms will react to.

If I simply say "Drive Safely" it's a rather perfunctory form of wording the message. It's quick, consisting of only two words. You likely would barely notice the message and you might also think that of course it's important to drive safely. You might ignore the message due to it seemingly being obvious, or you might notice it and think to yourself that it's kind of a handy reminder but that in the grand scheme of things it wasn't that necessary, at least not for you (maybe it was intended for riskier drivers, you assume).

Consider next the version that says "Thank You for Driving Safely." This message is somewhat longer, having now five words, and takes more effort to read. As you parse the words of the message, the opening element is that you are being thanked for something. We all like being thanked. What is it that you are being thanked for, you might wonder. You then get to the ending of the message and realize you are being thanked for driving safely.

Most people would then maybe get a small smile on their face and think that this was a mildly clever way to urge people to drive safely. By thanking people, it gets them to consider that they need to do something to get the thanks, and the thing they need to do is drive safely. In essence, the message tries to create a reciprocity with the person – you are getting a thank you handed to you, and you in return are supposed to do something, namely you are supposed to drive safely.

Suppose you opt to not drive safely? You've broken the convention of having been given something, the thanks, when it really was undeserved. In theory, you'll not want to break such a convention and therefore will be motivated to drive safely. I'd say that none of us will necessarily go out of our way to drive safely merely due to the aspect that you need to repay the thank you. On the other hand, maybe it will be enough of a social nudge that it puts you into a mental mindset of continuing to drive safely. It's not enough to force you into driving safely, but it might keep you going along as a safe driver.

What about the version that says "Drive Safely: It's the Law" and your reaction to it? In this version, you are being reminded to drive safely and then you are being forewarned that it is something you are supposed to do. You are told that the law requires you to drive safely. It's not really a choice per se, and instead it is the law. If you don't drive safely, you are a lawbreaker. You might get into legal trouble.

The version that says "Drive Safely or Get a Ticket" is similar to the version warning you about the law, and steps things up a further notch. If I tell you that something isn't lawful, you need to make a mental leap that if you break the law there are potentially adverse consequences. In the case of the version telling you straight out that you'll get a ticket, there's no ambiguity about the aspect that not only must you drive safely but indeed there is a distinct penalty for not doing so.

None of us likes getting a ticket. We've all had to deal with traffic tickets and the trauma of getting points dinged on our driving records, possibly having our car insurance rates hiked, and maybe needing to go to traffic school and suffer through boring hours of re-learning about driving. Yuk, nobody wants that. This version that mentions the ticket provides a specific adverse consequence if you don't comply with driving safely.

The word-for-word wording of the drive safely message is actually quite significant as to how the message will be received by others and whether they will be prompted to do anything because of the message.

I realize that some of you might say that it doesn't matter which of those wordings are used. Aren't we being rather tedious in parsing each such word? Seems like a lot of focus on something that otherwise doesn't need any attention. Well, you'd actually be somewhat mistaken in the assumption that those variants of wording do not make a difference. There are numerous psychology and cognition studies that show that the wording of a message can have an at times dramatic difference as to whether people notice the message and whether they take it to heart.

I'll concentrate herein on one such element that makes those messages so different in terms of impact, namely due to the use of reciprocity.

Reciprocity is a social norm. Cultural anthropologists suggest that it is a social norm that cuts across all cultures and all of time. In essence, we seem to have always believed in and accepted reciprocity in our dealings with others, whether we explicitly knew it or not.

I tell you that I'm going to help you with putting up a painting on your wall. You now feel as though you owe me something in return. It might be that you would pay me for helping you. Or, it could be something else such as you might do something for me, such as you offer to help me cook a meal. We're then balanced. I helped you with the painting, you helped me with the meal. In this case, we traded with each other, me giving you one type of service, and you providing in return to me some kind of service.

Of course, the trades could have been something other than a service. I help you put up the painting (I'm providing a service to you), and you then hand me a six pack of beer. In that case, I did a service for you, and you gave me a product in return (the beers). Maybe instead things started out that you gave me a six pack of beers (product) and I then offered to help put up your painting (a service). Or, it could be that you hand me the six pack of beers (product), and I hand you a pair of shoes (product).

In either case, one aspect is given to the other person, and the other person provides something in return. We seem to just know that this is the way the world works. Is it in our DNA? Is it something that we learn as children? It is both? There are arguments to be made about how it has come to be. Regardless of how it came to be, it exists and actually is a rather strong characteristic of our behavior.

Let's further unpack the nature of reciprocity.

I had mentioned that you gave me a six pack of beers and I then handed you a pair of shoes. Is that a fair trade? Maybe those shoes are old, worn out, and have holes in them. You might not need them and even if you needed them you might not want that particular pair of shoes. Seems like an uneven trade. You are likely to feel cheated and regret the trade. You might harbor a belief that I was not fair in my dealings with you. You might expect that I will give you something else of greater value to make-up for the lousy shoes.

On the other hand, maybe I'm not a beer drinker and so you're having given me beers seemed like an odd item to give to me. I might have thought that I'd give you an odd item in return. Perhaps in my mind, the trade was even. Meanwhile, in your mind, the trade was uneven.

There's another angle too as to whether the trade was intended as a positive one or something that is a negative one. We both are giving each other things of value and presumably done in a positive way. It could be a negative action kind of trade instead. I hit you in the head with my fist, and so you then kick me in the shin. Negative actions as a reciprocity. It's the old eye-for-an-eye kind of notion.

Time is a factor in reciprocity too. I help you put up your painting. Perhaps the meal you are going to help me cook is not going to take place until several months from today. That's going to be satisfactory in that we both at least know that there is a reciprocal arrangement underway.

If I help you with the painting, and there's no discussion about what you'll do for me, I'd walk away thinking that you owe me. You might also be thinking the same. Or, you could create an imbalance by not realizing you owe me, or maybe you are thinking that last year you help me put oil into my car and so that's what makes us even now on this most current trade.

Reciprocity can be dicey. There are ample ways that the whole thing can get combobbled. I do something for you, you don't do anything in return. I do something for you of value N, and you provide in return something of perceived value Y that is substantively less than N. I do something for you, and you pledge to do something for me that's a year from now, meanwhile I maybe feel cheated cause I didn't get more immediate value and also if you forget a year from now to make-up the trade then I forever might become upset. And so on.

I am assuming that you've encountered many of these kinds of reciprocity circumstances in your life time. You might not have realized at the time they were reciprocity situations. We often fall into them and aren't overtly aware of it.

One of the favorite examples about reciprocity in our daily lives involves the seemingly simple act of a waiter or waitress getting a tip after having served a meal. Studies show that if the server brings out the check and includes a mint on the tray holding the check, this has a tendency to increase the amount of the tip. The people that have eaten the meal and are getting ready to pay will feel as though they owe some kind of reciprocity due to the mint being there on the tray. Research indicates that the tip will definitely go up by a modest amount as a result of the act of providing the mint.

A savvy waiter or waitress can further exploit this reciprocity effect. If they look you in the eye and say that the mint was brought out just for you and your guests, this boosts the tip even more so. The rule of reciprocity comes to play since the value of the aspect being given has gone up, namely it was at first just any old mint and now it is a special mint just for you all, and thus the trade in kind by you is going to increase to match somewhat to the increase in value of the offering. The timing involved is crucial too, in that if the mint was given earlier in the meal, it would not have as great an impact as coming just at the time that the payment is going to be made.

As mentioned, reciprocity doesn't work on everyone in the same way.

The mint trick might not work on you, supposing you hate mints or you like them but perceive it of little value.

Or, if the waiter or waitress has irked you the entire meal, it is unlikely that the mint at the end is going to dig them out of a hole. In fact, sometimes when someone tries the reciprocity trick, it can backfire on them.

Upon seeing the mint and the server smiling at you, if you are already ticked-off about the meal and the service, it could actually cause you to go ballistic and decide to leave no tip or maybe ask for the manager and complain.

Here's a recap then about the reciprocity notion:

- Reciprocity is a social norm of tremendous power that seems to universally exist

- Often fall into a reciprocity and don't know it

- Usually a positive action needs to be traded for another in kind

- Usually a negative action needs to be traded for another in kind

- An imbalance in the perceived trades can mar the arrangement

- Trades can be services or products or combinations thereof

- Time can be a factor as to immediate, short-term, or long-term

What does this have to do with AI self-driving cars?

At the Cybernetic AI Self-Driving Car Institute, we are developing AI software for self-driving cars. One crucial aspect of the AI will be the interaction with the human occupants of the self-driving car, and as such, the AI should be crafted to leverage reciprocity.

One of the areas of open research and discussion involves the nature of the interaction between the AI of a self-driving car and the human occupants that will be using the self-driving car. Some AI developers with a narrow view seem to think that all that the interaction consists of would be the human occupants saying to drive them to the store or to home, and that's it. This is a naïve view. The human occupants are going to want to have the AI much abler to carry on a conversation.

You get into the AI self-driving car and decide you want to go to work. Almost as though you are giving an instruction to a GPS, you merely indicate the address of work, and the self-driving car then proceeds to drive you there. Suppose that during the journey, you want to get some coffee, doing so before you get to work. You would want to convey this interim destination to the AI.

Before the days of Alexa and Siri, we might have all accepted the idea that we might need to enter such instructions into an on-board computer tablet, but I think we are now expecting to be able to have a more natural audio interaction with the AI system. If you've gone to the trouble to buy an expensive and shiny AI self-driving car, you certainly would hope that some of the effort went into making the system interactive with the human occupants.

A barebones "conversational" AI might be this:

You: Take me to work.

AI self-driving car: Okay

What does the word "Okay" mean in this situation? Does it mean that the AI is acknowledging that you have said you want to go to work, but that it doesn't necessarily mean that the AI should immediately do so. Or, maybe it means that the AI is going to immediately start the self-driving car and drive you to work. Or, perhaps the AI misunderstood what you said and thought you said "I hate work" and therefore the AI is merely saying "Okay" as a placeholder word to seem responsive.

Let's try this again:

You: Take me to work.

AI self-driving car: Starting to your work now.

This is a little better since the AI has echoed back to you that you want to go to work, and furthermore it is stating when this action will occur, specifically that it will occur right away or now. This seems somewhat flat though. If you were conversing with a human chauffeur, they probably would be more embellishing in what they might say.

Here's another try:

You: Take me to work.

AI self-driving car: Good morning, I will head to your work at 1234 Lauren Street. Hope you will have a pleasant day at work!

This provides more specific feedback, including the work address, which helps to confirm that you really intended to go to work. It might be that you said the word "work" out of habit and meant to say "home" – by hearing the address it might cause you to realize that you had said the wrong word. The part of the message that says "good morning" and the other part that says "have a pleasant day" are added embellishments that presumably give a softer feeling to the messaging and makes things seem less robotic.

One criticism of having the AI utter "good morning" and "have a pleasant day" is that it implies perhaps that the AI actually means those things.

When I speak those words to you, you assume that I as a human have measured out those words and that I presumably know what it means to have a good morning, and so with my knowledge about the nature of mornings, I am genuinely hoping that you have a good one. If you see the words "good morning" written on a poster, you don't consider that the poster knows anything about the meaning of those words. When the AI system speaks those words, you are likely to be "fooled" into thinking that the AI system "understands" the nature of mornings and is basing those words on a sense of the world.

But, the AI of today is more akin to the poster, it is merely showcasing those words and does not yet (at least) comprehend the true meaning of those words.

Do we want the AI to seem to be more aware than it really is?

That's an important question. If the human occupants believe that the AI has some form of human awareness and knowledge, the human occupant might get themselves into a pickle by trying to converse with the AI system. Suppose the human starts to suffer a heart attack, and believes that the AI has human-like understanding, and so the human says "help, I'm having a heart attack" – if you said this to another adult, the human adult would likely realize that you are in trouble, they might call 911, they might try to aid you, etc.

The AI of today would not know what you've said per se. You though might have been misled into thinking that it would. If you believed that the AI was not so capable as a human, you might instead have uttered "take me to the nearest hospital" which then hopefully is similar to "take me to work" in that the system can parse the words and realize that it is a driving instruction. The AI would presumably then alter the driving path and instead drive the self-driving car to a nearby hospital.

This argument also comes up when AI developers put other human-like speaking mannerisms into their systems. Humans for example often will say "you know" or have pauses in their speaking or say "uh" while speaking. To-date, most of the AI natural language processing systems have generated spoken words that are streamlined and omit those human mannerisms. Lately, some AI developers have been including them. This gives the AI spoken words a closer to human-like feel.

Here's an example:

You: Take me to work.

AI self-driving car: Uh, Okay, sounds good... will do so.

The added elements to the response are going to suggest to the human listener that the AI is composing speech in a manner similar to a human. This anthropomorphizes the AI system, which as I've mentioned before can be good if you believe that's a desirable way to bond with the human occupants, but it can also be bad in that it can mislead as to what the AI system can and cannot really do and understand.

The joint interaction in a self-driving car between the human occupants and the AI are potentially going to involve life and death matters. This is an important point to keep in mind. If you are simply developing an online search engine that verbally interacts with humans or a system that can aid them in ordering toothbrushes and towels, whether the human believes that the AI is actually comprehending them is not particularly life threatening. In the case of a self-driving car, the human might need to offer insight to the AI about the driving task, or the AI might need to get input from the human about the driving task, any of which if improperly undertaken could have dire consequences.

This then takes us to the reciprocity aspects.

Should the AI system of the self-driving car carry on conversations that also invoke the use of reciprocity? If you are of a mind that the AI should not overinflate what it can actually comprehend, you'd probably say that it should not also imbue reciprocity. If you are seeking to have the AI appear as sentient as it can, the use of reciprocity would be a core element to achieve that sense, since it is so common among humans and part-and-parcel of our daily lives.

Here's an example:

You: Take me to work.

AI self-driving car: Happy to take you to work. Please make sure to keep your seat belts on.

You likely can detect the subtle reciprocity involved in the dialogue. The AI implies that it is doing something for the human occupant, taking them to work, and the punch-up is that the AI is "happy" to do so. This creates a human-like aspect as though the AI was doing this as a service for you. The trade is that in return, you are being asked to keep your seat belts on.

If we strip away the reciprocity, we'd get something like this instead:

You: Take me to work.

AI self-driving car: Okay. Keep your seat belts on.

This version is similar to the earlier example about the drive safely message. We've now got a plainer and straightforward kind of instruction or maybe even an edict, which was the same with the "drive safely" message. The "happy to take you to work" was more akin to the "thank you for driving safely" message that created a kind of quid-pro-quo element to the dialogue.

If we make the messaging more along the negative side, it might be something like this:

You: Take me to work.

AI self-driving car: Okay. Keep your seat belts on or I'll stop the car and you won't get to work on time.

Whoa! This sounds like some kind of fierce AI that is threatening you.

There are AI developers that would argue that this message is actually better than the others because it makes abundantly clear the adverse consequence if the human does not wear their seat belts. Yes, it's true that it does spell out the consequences, but it also perhaps sets up a "relationship" with the human occupant that's going to be an angry one. It sets the tone in a manner that might cause the human to consider in what manner they want to respond back to the AI (angrily!).

If the AI system is intended to interact with the human occupants in a near-natural way, the role of reciprocity needs to be considered.

It is a common means of human to human interaction. Likewise, the AI self-driving car will be undertaking the driving task and some kind of give-and-take with the human occupants is likely to occur.

We believe that as AI natural language processing capabilities get better, incorporating reciprocity will further enhance the seeming natural part of natural language processing. It is prudent though to be cautious in overstepping what can be achieved and the life-and-death consequences of human and AI interaction in a self-driving car context needs to be kept in mind.

CHAPTER 13

PET MODE AND

AI SELF-DRIVING CARS

CHAPTER 13

PET MODE AND
AI SELF-DRIVING CARS

What is the most popular type of pet in the United States?

Kind of a trick question, I suppose, since you undoubtedly first thought of dogs or cats. The answer is that freshwater fish are the most popular pet, consisting of an estimated 142 million of them.

I'll give you another try. Are there more dogs or cats as pets in the United States? Turns out that cats are about 88 million and dogs are about 75 million, so cats come out to be the victor in terms of popularity by count. Dog owners would likely argue though that in spite of there being more cats, maybe we should count popularity by some other factor (Weight? Friendliness?) and dogs would be the top dog, so to speak.

Putting aside the debate about which kind of pet is the best or worst, it can be surprising to realize how big the pet market is. An estimated 68% of United States households have a pet. The spending on pets in the United States is an estimated $70 billion or more. That's a lot of money. That's a lot of households. That's a lot of people that either own a pet or maybe enjoy being with someone else's pet. If tomorrow somehow all pets suddenly disappeared, think about how it would impact people's lives and how much we've come to rely upon having at the ready our pets.

I used to have a dog. I used to have a cat. I mention both of them since some of you might think I'm more of a dog-person or a cat-person – I'm an equal opportunity pet owner (I've also had freshwater fish, birds, reptiles, etc.). For my dog, I would occasionally take him down to the beach for a romp on the sand. He loved to run around and chase the birds and chase the waves as they crashed on the beach. It was quite a workout for him and he'd be tuckered out by the time we got back home.

Getting him to the beach was a bit of a hassle. At the house he roamed free. When I took him in the car, I'd put on his leash (he usually assumed he was going for a walk around the block), and then I'd put him into the backseat of the car. Actually, the moment I opened the door of the car he knew what was going to happen next and with grand delight he'd leap into the car. I'd use the leash to loosely tie him down so that he couldn't wander throughout the car. As with most dogs, he enjoyed putting his nose outside the window to smell the cacophony of odors as we drove to the beach and so I always cracked open the window for him.

Excitability would sometimes get the better of him while in the car. This meant that there might be biological emissions during his time in the car, including excrement and urine, which obviously is not what one usually hopes to have in their car. Anticipating these moments, I put towels in the car and a blanket upon which I hoped he would generally stay, plus I tried to train him to "hold it" until we got out of the car at our destination. The return trip from the beach was similar to the trip to the beach, except that he usually was tired and would lay down in the car. This had its own disadvantages because he often had sand on him and other muck that he might have encountered during his beach romp.

The joy of playing with him at the beach, and seeing his joy of being at the beach, made the whole gauntlet of steps to do the drive worthwhile. For my cat, trips in the car were almost always solely to take the cat to the vet. Unfortunately, the cat figured this out. As a result, the moment that I started to make motions that I was going to take the cat to the vet, the cat would hide or play hard to get. I tried a few times to let the cat be loose in the car, having a leash similar to what I had done with the dog. The cat though hated being in the car and would scratch and hiss, so the best means of transport ended up involving the use of a pet carrier for the cat (it wasn't so much the car that the cat hated, as it was the realization that it was time to see the vet).

Whenever you have an animal inside a car, it can be a dicey proposition.

As the driver of the car, you certainly don't want the animal to interfere with your driving. A cat that's allowed to wander anywhere within the confines of the car could suddenly jump in your lap and you'd be so startled that you'd maybe steer the car off a cliff. A dog that can move around could get angry at a dog on the street and start barking, maybe distracting you, doing so just as you are making a right turn and perhaps you inadvertently hit a nearby pedestrian.

If you are transporting freshwater fish, I suppose it's less likely of something going amiss in the car, though if you have them in a simple fish bowl, and if you happen to hit the brakes while driving, they might go flying throughout your car, and in so doing disturb you that you become distracted from the driving task. Anything can happen.

A rule-of-thumb would seem to be that for any animals inside a car, it's best to control them in a manner that they cannot disturb the driving of the car.

I had a friend that would carry his dog in his arms and ride as a front-seat passenger in someone else's car. One day, the dog freaked out when another car honked its horn, which caused my friend to reflexively try to re-grab his dog, which caused my friend to flail around in the passenger seat, which then he unintentionally hit the driver, and the driver of the car then rammed into a car ahead of them. Quite a story to tell the police or the insurance company.

The story is helpful because it highlights that there is a range of "control" that one might have with the animal. Some people tie down their pet while it's in the car and try to immobilize it from impacting the driver. Some think that verbal commands alone will keep the animal from getting out of hand. My friend thought he could just hold his pet in his arms. My having put the cat into a pet carrier pretty much prevented the cat from disturbing my driving, though the cat meowing and hissing did admittedly perhaps distract me somewhat from being fully attentive to the driving task.

Here's some possibilities that we want to presumably avoid when transporting an animal inside a car:

- Animal endangers the driver

- Animal endangers other occupants

- Animal endangers the car

- Animal endangers itself

- Animal endangers others outside the car

I saw a dog leap out a window of a car one day and chase after a person that the dog apparently disliked, thus, it's conceivable that an animal could endangers others outside of the car. At supermarkets, you sometimes see people that have parked their cars and left an angry dog in it, which when people walk past the car, the dog tries to take a bite of them. Not good for anyone, humans nor pet.

There have been cases of animals inside a car that wrecked the interior of the car. I even heard about one time that a person left their engine running, got out of the car to do some quick task, and the dog somehow bumped into the transmission knob and the car went into drive. Luckily, miraculously, I don't believe anyone was hurt in that instance. I did hear though that the dog went to the Department of Motor Vehicles (DMV) in hopes of getting a driver's license. Well, maybe not.

I know that some people get upset when I say that you should control your pet while it's in your car. They argue with me that if the animal is domesticated, there should not be any concern about controlling the animal. Only if the animal is a wild animal do they think that there's any need to be overtly thinking about controlling the animal. I don't want pet owners to get upset with me, but I'll just point out that even the most domesticated animal still has animal instincts and reactions.

In my view, you can't be too careful, especially when it comes to putting an animal into the rather confined space of a car and once the car gets into motion you are opening up a can of worms. It can be an explosive and dangerous combination.

Pets can do any of these things:

- Become scared
- Get startled
- Become upset
- Get angry
- Try to run or scamper
- Bite
- Become confused
- Scratch
- Etc.

If anything, I'm often concerned not just for the human driver or the human occupants, but also for the animal itself. When someone thinks they are doing a good thing by letting their dog roam freely in a moving car, they aren't thinking about the harm that can come to the dog. Suppose the driver suddenly hits the brakes? That dog is going to go flying in the car and possibly get injured or killed by hitting something in the car or maybe even getting thrown outside of the car. Most states have various laws and regulations about restraining your pet while it is in your moving car, for its safety and your safety.

What does this have to do with AI self-driving cars?

At the Cybernetic AI Self-Driving Car Institute, we are developing AI software for self-driving cars. This includes encompassing various "edge" problems such as the transporting of pets (animals) while in an

AI self-driving car.

Let's consider some of the aspects involved in this edge problem. I call it an edge problem because it is considered by most of the auto makers and tech firms as something outside the core of what an AI self-driving car is supposed to do. They are focused on getting the AI to drive the car. The aspects of dealing with any pets inside a car is considered secondary and much lower on the list of crucial things to get done.

Let's also define what is meant by an AI self-driving car. There are various levels of self-driving cars. At the topmost level, Level 5, it's a self-driving car for which the AI can fully drive the car. This means that there is no human driver required in the self-driving car at a Level 5. For the levels less than a Level 5, there is a need to have a human driver present. The human driver and the AI are considered co-sharing the driving task, though the human is also considered ultimately responsible for the actions of the car. This notion of co-sharing the driving task is something I've mentioned many times is raft with various drawbacks.

In the case of an AI self-driving car that is less-than a Level 5, there needs to be a human driver at the ready to drive the car. This implies that if you do have an animal in the car, it's similar to the situation today of having an animal in a conventional car. Anything that the animal does that disturbs the human driver can have adverse and dire consequences.

I realize you might be thinking that if the AI is co-sharing the driving task, why doesn't it just wrench control from the human driver if the human driver suddenly becomes unable to do the driving task.

This has several problems.

One is that how will the AI realize that it is best to take control from the human driver? Even if the AI is detecting whether the human driver has their hands on the wheel or maybe via a camera whether the human is looking forward at the road, trying to judge when it is appropriate to take over control is not very transparent. Imagine too if the AI does take over control and it turns out that the human was still in control, but that the AI now maybe is going to take an untoward action since it doesn't know what the human driver was intending to do.

You could even get into a tug of war between the AI and the human, trying to take control from each other. I suppose you might contend that if the human tries to take control back, the AI should relent. But, suppose the human doesn't know now what the AI was intending to do, and so the human puts the car into an untoward posture. Or, maybe the human takes back control, but then let's say the dog in the car jumps on the human a second time and it is necessary for the AI to once again take control. Meanwhile, maybe you've used a rule that if the AI takes control, and the human takes it back, leave the control with the human, avoiding a tug of war. That wouldn't work out in all cases.

You might say that if the AI is indeed watching what's going on in the self-driving car, maybe it should be sharp enough that it can figure out that say a dog is loose or cat is loose. Yes, you could potentially have the machine learning recognition that would be programmed for this, but it is much subtler than you might think. Generally, it would require some kind of common sense reasoning to try and decide whether the dogs or cats are doing something relatively safe or unsafe.

Another perspective is that you might have the human driver tell the AI to take over control. This would be similar to when you initiate say Alexa and so you say a code word, "Alexa" and then you provide some kind of command. It could be that the AI self-driving car has a code word, let's use "Lance," and then after you say that word you can tell it to take over control of the driving task. I realize that some of you will say that suppose a child in the car suddenly yells out the code word and then all of a sudden the AI construes whatever is said next as a command ("go off a cliff"). Some counter-argue that the AI could be using a voice fingerprint identify capability such that it would only recognize and acknowledge the human driver's voice at the time of the driving task.

In recap, here's some aspects involved:

- AI tries to ascertain if an animal is amuck

- AI potentially takes over driving task if human driver seems unable

- Human driver can signal to the AI to take over the driving task

- Human driver can signal to take back the driving task or refuse to give it up

- Miscommunication in the co-sharing could have dire consequences

- Misunderstanding in the co-sharing could have dire consequences

One approach too involves having the AI be a kind of an alert monitor about the animal in the self-driving car. In essence, the AI could be placed into "pet mode" and be ready for the particular dynamics of having a pet inside the self-driving car. This pet mode could be initiated overtly by the human occupant telling the AI to go into pet mode, or it could be figured out by the AI via machine learning recognition of the "objects" inside of the self-driving car (and possibly with a confirmation to the human driver that indeed there is an animal on-board).

Part of the "pet mode" could be that the AI would be on the watch on behalf of the human driver about things that the pet is doing. It would be akin to having a passenger in the car that can tell you that the dog just chewed the backseat armrest, or the cat is curled up in a ball on the floor. With a human passenger, they would be able though to take physical action when needed and help restrain the animal, but there's not much the AI of the self-driving car can do in that regard. Instead, the AI would be devoted to warning the human driver about what the animal is doing, and being another pair of eyes, so to speak, while the human is presumably watching the road and being at the ready for the driving task.

You could potentially have the AI try to talk to the animal. Perhaps your pet dog has been trained to listen to the AI of your self-driving car. The AI then could potentially tell the dog to sit down or get into the backseat. I realize this seems kind of wild as an approach, but as you'll see in a moment, maybe it's not as crazy as it seems.

Let's now consider the use of "pet mode" for a Level 5 self-driving car. In the case of the Level 5, the AI is doing all the driving. There is no human driver. This is handy because it implies the animal is unable to distract the driver. Whatever the animal does, the AI is still going to be able to drive the car.

The only way the animal presumably can disrupt the driving would be if it is able to damage something inside the self-driving car that could hamper the AI or the car itself. Suppose that there is wiring just under the dashboard and somehow the dog gets to it and chews through those cables. If they are involved in the electronics of the car and any kind of driving related task, it could be disruptive to the AI and the car integrity.

This then brings up facets about the interior design of the self-driving car. It is generally envisioned that since there is no longer a need for a human driver in a Level 5 self-driving car, we can redesign the interior compartment of the self-driving car. No need to have a seat facing forward in the same place that today's driver seats reside. Instead, the compartment can be perhaps seats that swivel and face each other. Or, maybe seats that can recline fully so you can sleep in your self-driving car when you want to do so. With the potential of true AI self-driving cars being used non-stop 24x7, it is presumed that people will likely sleep while on their way to work or on trips to visit in-laws, etc.

When redesigning the interior of cars to be suitable as a self-driving car, one additional consideration will be the nature of the occupants and what they might do inside the self-driving car. If you are going to put your children into a true AI self-driving car in the morning so that they will be driven to school, doing so without any adult supervision inside the self-driving car, you want to know that the children hopefully cannot harm themselves by poking around within the interior of the car. Today's cars leave all sorts of metal joints and prods fully exposed inside the compartment, which a small child without supervision could easily harm themselves on. The same could be said about pets that are unsupervised.

Indeed, when you consider that 68% of U.S. households have pets, and once there are true AI self-driving cars prevalent, just imagine how many of these households will opt to send their pet by itself in the family AI self-driving car to go visit the vet. Or go visit grandma. Or go to a pet playground where there is someone to supervise your pet, and then they put your pet back into your AI self-driving car, which comes to work to pick you up at the end of the day, and your joyful dog is right there to greet you. No need to wait until you get home to get some hugs and kisses from your beloved pet.

The redesign of the interior of a car should take into account the notion that today's designs are inherently dangerous and assume that whomever is in the car will be somewhat supervised. True AI self-driving cars won't necessarily have an adult in the car to undertake supervision of children and nor pets. Overall, this implies that the interior has to be made safety proof with regard to whomever is inside the self-driving car. There shouldn't be any easy way to cut yourself. There shouldn't be any easy way to undermine the capabilities of the self-driving car by hitting something or chewing on something.

This does not mean that the interior needs to be a steel tank or barren fortress. The auto maker can provide various covers and shields to allow for a relatively impervious interior. I'd even assert that if the auto makers don't do so, a thriving third-party market will likely develop to outfit your interior compartment so that it is safer for the transport of children, pets, etc.

I had mentioned earlier that the AI might be made to talk to the pet. Suppose your pet will be in the true AI self-driving car for an hour or two, perhaps taking a lengthy journey. That's a long time for your pet to be alone. The AI could be talking to the pet, maybe playing music, or otherwise try to comfort the animal. Given that there are likely cameras pointing inward, you can do a Skype like chat with your pet, and the inside of the AI self-driving car is likely to have screens, used usually to show movies or do your digital work. Your pet could see you, you could see your pet, and try to comfort your pet during part of its journey in the self-driving car.

I had mentioned earlier that the seats in a true AI self-driving car might swivel and there might be other variations in terms of configuring the internal compartment. For those that have pets, there might be ways to re-configure the inside compartment to allow for taking out the seats and allowing the pet to wander around inside the car.

Perhaps there might be a special leash or restraint system that keeps the animal relatively safe, but also allows for open movement while in the car, most of the time (the restraint system might opt to more strongly restrain the animal if getting into rough traffic, or maybe if the pet is getting out-of-hand). Anyway, you can just see the ads now, the XYZ auto maker comes out with a pet friendly AI self-driving car and tries to lure buyers that have pets – could be a sizable segment of the market.

It is anticipated that the advent of true AI self-driving car is going to be a tremendous boon to the ridesharing industry. People will buy a self-driving car, realize that it can be used 24x7, and opt to rent it out while they are at work or asleep. Other people will buy a self-driving car solely as a ridesharing revenue maker and not even use it for personal purposes. We're head toward a ridesharing economy, or ridesharing-as-a-service world.

That being the case, what about pets? People are going to want to have their pets go lots of places that right now involves too much of a hassle for them to drive their pet to, and yet with a true AI self-driving car it could be a breeze. Some ridesharing services might tout that they have pet-devoted AI self-driving cars, ready for the transporting of your favorite dog, cat, or fish. I've already predicted that with the advent of AI self-driving cars we are going to see all sorts of induced demand. This is demand for using a car that otherwise today is suppressed or that people don't even think about currently.

I began this discussion by pointing out that we today spend $70 billion on our pets, doing so for pet food, for pet toys, for pet care, and the like. It seems logical and inevitable that true AI self-driving cars are going to ultimately intersect with our desire to have pets.

Right now, if I told you that someday your pet will be driven around in an otherwise empty car, you'd think I was loco or that it would have to be some crazy rich person that is spending way too much money on their pet. In the future, the prevalence of AI self-driving cars will open the avenue for considering ridesharing involving our pets. Easily, readily, at a low cost. It's going to happen.

The idea of a pet mode for an AI self-driving car is not particularly farfetched if you have a long-term view, at least that's what we say.

Well, I suppose it could be that me and my team just love our pets so much that we insist on somehow getting them involved in AI self-driving cars. I wonder if I could train a dog to do AI coding? Or, would a cat do a better job at it? It's hard to say.

APPENDIX

APPENDIX A

TEACHING WITH THIS MATERIAL

The material in this book can be readily used either as a supplemental to other content for a class, or it can also be used as a core set of textbook material for a specialized class. Classes where this material is most likely used include any classes at the college or university level that want to augment the class by offering thought provoking and educational essays about AI and self-driving cars.

In particular, here are some aspects for class use:

o   <u>Computer Science</u>. Studying AI, autonomous vehicles, etc.

o   <u>Business</u>. Exploring technology and it adoption for business.

o   <u>Sociology</u>. Sociological views on the adoption and advancement of technology.

Specialized classes at the undergraduate and graduate level can also make use of this material.

For each chapter, consider whether you think the chapter provides material relevant to your course topic. There is plenty of opportunity to get the students thinking about the topic and force them to decide whether they agree or disagree with the points offered and positions taken. I would also encourage you to have the students do additional research beyond the chapter material presented (I provide next some suggested assignments they can do).

RESEARCH ASSIGNMENTS ON THESE TOPICS

Your students can find background material on these topics, doing so in various business and technical publications. I list below the top ranked AI related journals. For business publications, I would suggest the usual culprits such as the Harvard Business Review, Forbes, Fortune, WSJ, and the like.

Here are some suggestions of homework or projects that you could assign to students:

a) Assignment for foundational AI research topic: Research and prepare a paper and a presentation on a specific aspect of Deep AI, Machine Learning, ANN, etc. The paper should cite at least 3 reputable sources. Compare and contrast to what has been stated in this book.

b) Assignment for the Self-Driving Car topic: Research and prepare a paper and Self-Driving Cars. Cite at least 3 reputable sources and analyze the characterizations. Compare and contrast to what has been stated in this book.

c) Assignment for a Business topic: Research and prepare a paper and a presentation on businesses and advanced technology. What is hot, and what is not? Cite at least 3 reputable sources. Compare and contrast to the depictions in this book.

d) Assignment to do a Startup: Have the students prepare a paper about how they might startup a business in this realm. They must submit a sound Business Plan for the startup. They could also be asked to present their Business Plan and so should also have a presentation deck to coincide with it.

You can certainly adjust the aforementioned assignments to fit to your particular needs and the class structure. You'll notice that I ask for 3 reputable cited sources for the paper writing based assignments. I usually steer students toward "reputable" publications, since otherwise they will cite some oddball source that has no credentials other than that they happened to write something and post it onto the Internet. You can define "reputable" in whatever way you prefer, for example some faculty think Wikipedia is not reputable while others believe it is reputable and allow students to cite it.

The reason that I usually ask for at least 3 citations is that if the student only does one or two citations they usually settle on whatever they happened to find the fastest. By requiring three citations, it usually seems to force them to look around, explore, and end-up probably finding five or more, and then whittling it down to 3 that they will actually use.

I have not specified the length of their papers, and leave that to you to tell the students what you prefer. For each of those assignments, you could end-up with a short one to two pager, or you could do a dissertation length paper. Base the length on whatever best fits for your class, and the credit amount of the assignment within the context of the other grading metrics you'll be using for the class.

I mention in the assignments that they are to do a paper and prepare a presentation. I usually try to get students to present their work. This is a good practice for what they will do in the business world. Most of the time, they will be required to prepare an analysis and present it. If you don't have the class time or inclination to have the students present, then you can of course cut out the aspect of them putting together a presentation.

If you want to point students toward highly ranked journals in AI, here's a list of the top journals as reported by *various citation counts sources* (this list changes year to year):

- o   Communications of the ACM
- o   Artificial Intelligence
- o   Cognitive Science
- o   IEEE Transactions on Pattern Analysis and Machine Intelligence
- o   Foundations and Trends in Machine Learning
- o   Journal of Memory and Language
- o   Cognitive Psychology
- o   Neural Networks
- o   IEEE Transactions on Neural Networks and Learning Systems
- o   IEEE Intelligent Systems
- o   Knowledge-based Systems

GUIDE TO USING THE CHAPTERS

For each of the chapters, I provide next some various ways to use the chapter material. You can assign the tasks as individual homework assignments, or the tasks can be used with team projects for the class. You can easily layout a series of assignments, such as indicating that the students are to do item "a" below for say Chapter 1, then "b" for the next chapter of the book, and so on.

a) What is the main point of the chapter and describe in your own words the significance of the topic,

b) Identify at least two aspects in the chapter that you agree with, and support your concurrence by providing at least one other outside researched item as support; make sure to explain your basis for disagreeing with the aspects,

c) Identify at least two aspects in the chapter that you disagree with, and support your disagreement by providing at least one other outside researched item as support; make sure to explain your basis for disagreeing with the aspects,

d) Find an aspect that was not covered in the chapter, doing so by conducting outside research, and then explain how that aspect ties into the chapter and what significance it brings to the topic,

e) Interview a specialist in industry about the topic of the chapter, collect from them their thoughts and opinions, and readdress the chapter by citing your source and how they compared and contrasted to the material,

f) Interview a relevant academic professor or researcher in a college or university about the topic of the chapter, collect from them their thoughts and opinions, and readdress the chapter by citing your source and how they compared and contrasted to the material,

g) Try to update a chapter by finding out the latest on the topic, and ascertain whether the issue or topic has now been solved or whether it is still being addressed, explain what you come up with.

The above are all ways in which you can get the students of your class involved in considering the material of a given chapter. You could mix things up by having one of those above assignments per each week, covering the chapters over the course of the semester or quarter.

As a reminder, here are the chapters of the book and you can select whichever chapters you find most valued for your particular class:

Chapter Title

1 Eliot Framework for AI Self-Driving Cars 15

2 Start-ups and AI Self-Driving Cars 29

3 Code Obfuscation and AI Self-Driving Cars 45

4 Hyperlanes and AI Self-Driving Cars 59

5 Passenger Panic Inside an AI Self-Driving Car 73

6 Tech Stockholm Syndrome and Self-Driving Cars 89

7 Paralysis and AI Self-Driving Cars 103

8 Ugly Zones and AI Self-Driving Cars 119

9 Ridesharing and AI Self-Driving Cars 133

10 Multi-Party Privacy and AI Self-Driving Cars 147

11 Chaff Bugs and AI Self-Driving Cars 163

12 Social Reciprocity and AI Self-Driving Cars 177

13 Pet Mode and AI Self-Driving Cars 193

Companion Book By This Author

Advances in AI and Autonomous Vehicles: Cybernetic Self-Driving Cars

Practical Advances in Artificial Intelligence (AI) and Machine Learning

by

Dr. Lance B. Eliot, MBA, PhD

Chapter Title

1 Genetic Algorithms for Self-Driving Cars

2 Blockchain for Self-Driving Cars

3 Machine Learning and Data for Self-Driving Cars

4 Edge Problems at Core of True Self-Driving Cars

5 Solving the Roundabout Traversal Problem for SD Cars

6 Parallel Parking Mindless Task for SD Cars: Step It Up

7 Caveats of Open Source for Self-Driving Cars

8 Catastrophic Cyber Hacking of Self-Driving Cars

9 Conspicuity for Self-Driving Cars

10 Accident Scene Traversal for Self-Driving Cars

11 Emergency Vehicle Awareness for Self-Driving Cars

12 Are Left Turns Right for Self-Driving Cars

13 Going Blind: When Sensors Fail on Self-Driving Cars

14 Roadway Debris Cognition for Self-Driving Cars

15 Avoiding Pedestrian Roadkill by Self-Driving Cars

16 When Accidents Happen to Self-Driving Cars

17 Illegal Driving for Self-Driving Cars

18 Making AI Sense of Road Signs

19 Parking Your Car the AI Way

20 Not Fast Enough: Human Factors in Self-Driving Cars

21 State of Government Reporting on Self-Driving Cars

22 The Head Nod Problem for Self-Driving Cars

23 CES Reveals Self-Driving Car Differences

This title is available via Amazon and other book sellers

Companion Book By This Author

Self-Driving Cars:
"The Mother of All AI Projects"

by Dr. Lance B. Eliot, MBA, PhD

Chapter Title

1 Grand Convergence Explains Rise of Self-Driving Cars

2 Here is Why We Need to Call Them Self-Driving Cars

3 Richter Scale for Levels of Self-Driving Cars

4 LIDAR as Secret Sauce for Self-Driving Cars

5 Pied Piper Approach to SD Car-Following

6 Sizzle Reel Trickery for AI Self-Driving Car Hype

7 Roller Coaster Public Perception of Self-Driving Cars

8 Brainless Self-Driving Shuttles Not Same as SD Cars

9 First Salvo Class Action Lawsuits for Defective SD Cars

10 AI Fake News About Self-Driving Cars

11 Rancorous Ranking of Self-Driving Cars

12 Product Liability for Self-Driving Cars

13 Humans Colliding with Self-Driving Cars

14 Elderly Boon or Bust for Self-Driving Cars

15 Simulations for Self-Driving Cars: Machine Learning

16 DUI Drunk Driving by Self-Driving Cars

17 Ten Human-Driving Foibles: Deep Learning

18 Art of Defensive Driving is Key to Self-Driving Cars

19 Cyclops Approach to AI Self-Driving Cars is Myopic

20 Steering Wheel Gets Self-Driving Car Attention

21 Remote Piloting is a Self-Driving Car Crutch

22 Self-Driving Cars: Zero Fatalities, Zero Chance

23 Goldrush: Self-Driving Car Lawsuit Bonanza Ahead

24 Road Trip Trickery for Self-Driving Trucks and Cars

25 Ethically Ambiguous Self-Driving Car

This title is available via Amazon and other book sellers

Companion Book By This Author

Innovation and Thought Leadership on Self-Driving Driverless Cars

by Dr. Lance B. Eliot, MBA, PhD

Chapter Title

1 Sensor Fusion for Self-Driving Cars

2 Street Scene Free Space Detection Self-Driving Cars

3 Self-Awareness for Self-Driving Cars

4 Cartographic Trade-offs for Self-Driving Cars

5 Toll Road Traversal for Self-Driving Cars

6 Predictive Scenario Modeling for Self-Driving Cars

7 Selfishness for Self-Driving Cars

8 Leap Frog Driving for Self-Driving Cars

9 Proprioceptive IMU's for Self-Driving Cars

10 Robojacking of Self-Driving Cars

11 Self-Driving Car Moonshot and Mother of AI Projects

12 Marketing of Self-Driving Cars

13 Are Airplane Autopilots Same as Self-Driving Cars

14 Savvy Self-Driving Car Regulators: Marc Berman

15 Event Data Recorders (EDR) for Self-Driving Cars

16 Looking Behind You for Self-Driving Cars

17 In-Car Voice Commands NLP for Self-Driving Cars

18 When Self-Driving Cars Get Pulled Over by a Cop

19 Brainjacking Neuroprosthetus Self-Driving Cars

This title is available via Amazon and other book sellers

Companion Book By This Author

New Advances in AI Autonomous Driverless Cars Self-Driving Cars

by Dr. Lance B. Eliot, MBA, PhD

Chapter Title

1 Eliot Framework for AI Self-Driving Cars

2 Self-Driving Cars Learning from Self-Driving Cars

3 Imitation as Deep Learning for Self-Driving Cars

4 Assessing Federal Regulations for Self-Driving Cars

5 Bandwagon Effect for Self-Driving Cars

6 AI Backdoor Security Holes for Self-Driving Cars

7 Debiasing of AI for Self-Driving Cars

8 Algorithmic Transparency for Self-Driving Cars

9 Motorcycle Disentanglement for Self-Driving Cars

10 Graceful Degradation Handling of Self-Driving Cars

11 AI for Home Garage Parking of Self-Driving Cars

12 Motivational AI Irrationality for Self-Driving Cars

13 Curiosity as Cognition for Self-Driving Cars

14 Automotive Recalls of Self-Driving Cars

15 Internationalizing AI for Self-Driving Cars

16 Sleeping as AI Mechanism for Self-Driving Cars

17 Car Insurance Scams and Self-Driving Cars

18 U-Turn Traversal AI for Self-Driving Cars

19 Software Neglect for Self-Driving Cars

This title is available via Amazon and other book sellers

Companion Book By This Author

Introduction to
Driverless Self-Driving Cars

by Dr. Lance B. Eliot, MBA, PhD

Chapter Title

1 Self-Driving Car Moonshot: Mother of All AI Projects
2 Grand Convergence Leads to Self-Driving Cars
3 Why They Should Be Called Self-Driving Cars
4 Richter Scale for Self-Driving Car Levels
5 LIDAR for Self-Driving Cars
6 Overall Framework for Self-Driving Cars
7 Sensor Fusion is Key for Self-Driving Cars
8 Humans Not Fast Enough for Self-Driving Cars
9 Solving Edge Problems of Self-Driving Cars
10 Graceful Degradation for Faltering Self-Driving Cars
11 Genetic Algorithms for Self-Driving Cars
12 Blockchain for Self-Driving Cars
13 Machine Learning and Data for Self-Driving Cars
14 Cyber-Hacking of Self-Driving Cars
15 Sensor Failures in Self-Driving Cars
16 When Accidents Happen to Self-Driving Cars
17 Backdoor Security Holes in Self-Driving Cars
18 Future Brainjacking for Self-Driving Cars
19 Internationalizing Self-Driving Cars
20 Are Airline Autopilots Same as Self-Driving Cars
21 Marketing of Self-Driving Cars
22 Fake News about Self-Driving Cars
23 Product Liability for Self-Driving Cars
24 Zero Fatalities Zero Chance for Self-Driving Cars
25 Road Trip Trickery for Self-Driving Cars
26 Ethical Issues of Self-Driving Cars
27 Ranking of Self-Driving Cars
28 Induced Demand Driven by Self-Driving Cars

This title is available via Amazon and other book sellers

<u>Companion Book By This Author</u>
Autonomous Vehicle Driverless Self-Driving Cars and Artificial Intelligence
by Dr. Lance B. Eliot, MBA, PhD

<u>Chapter Title</u>

1 Eliot Framework for AI Self-Driving Cars

2 Rocket Man Drivers and AI Self-Driving Cars

3 Occam's Razor Crucial for AI Self-Driving Cars

4 Simultaneous Local/Map (SLAM) for Self-Driving Cars

5 Swarm Intelligence for AI Self-Driving Cars

6 Biomimicry and Robomimicry for Self-Driving Cars

7 Deep Compression/Pruning for AI Self-Driving Cars

8 Extra-Scenery Perception for AI Self-Driving Cars

9 Invasive Curve and AI Self-Driving Cars

10 Normalization of Deviance and AI Self-Driving Cars

11 Groupthink Dilemma for AI Self-Driving Cars

12 Induced Demand Driven by AI Self-Driving Cars

13 Compressive Sensing for AI Self-Driving Cars

14 Neural Layer Explanations for AI Self-Driving Cars

15 Self-Adapting Resiliency for AI Self-Driving Cars

16 Prisoner's Dilemma and AI Self-Driving Cars

17 Turing Test and AI Self-Driving Cars

18 Support Vector Machines for AI Self-Driving Cars

19 "Expert Systems and AI Self-Driving Cars" by Michael Eliot

This title is available via Amazon and other book sellers

Transformative Artificial Intelligence
Driverless Self-Driving Cars

by Dr. Lance B. Eliot, MBA, PhD

Chapter Title

1 Eliot Framework for AI Self-Driving Cars

2 Kinetosis Anti-Motion Sickness for Self-Driving Cars

3 Rain Driving for Self-Driving Cars

4 Edge Computing for Self-Driving Cars

5 Motorcycles as AI Self-Driving Vehicles

6 CAPTCHA Cyber-Hacking and Self-Driving Cars

7 Probabilistic Reasoning for Self-Driving Cars

8 Proving Grounds for Self-Driving Cars

9 Frankenstein and AI Self-Driving Cars

10 Omnipresence for Self-Driving Cars

11 Looking Behind You for Self-Driving Cars

12 Over-The-Air (OTA) Updating for Self-Driving Cars

13 Snow Driving for Self-Driving Cars

14 Human-Aided Training for Self-Driving Cars

15 Privacy for Self-Driving Cars

16 Transduction Vulnerabilities for Self-Driving Cars

17 Conversations Computing and Self-Driving Cars

18 Flying Debris and Self-Driving Cars

19 Citizen AI for Self-Driving Cars

This title is available via Amazon and other book sellers

Companion Book By This Author

Disruptive Artificial Intelligence and Driverless Self-Driving Cars

by Dr. Lance B. Eliot, MBA, PhD

Chapter Title

1 Eliot Framework for AI Self-Driving Cars

2 Maneuverability and Self-Driving Cars

3 Common Sense Reasoning and Self-Driving Cars

4 Cognition Timing and Self-Driving Cars

5 Speed Limits and Self-Driving Vehicles

6 Human Back-up Drivers and Self-Driving Cars

7 Forensic Analysis Uber and Self-Driving Cars

8 Power Consumption and Self-Driving Cars

9 Road Rage and Self-Driving Cars

10 Conspiracy Theories and Self-Driving Cars

11 Fear Landscape and Self-Driving Cars

12 Pre-Mortem and Self-Driving Cars

13 Kits and Self-Driving Cars

This title is available via Amazon and other book sellers

<u>Companion Book By This Author</u>

State-of-the-Art
AI Driverless Self-Driving Cars

by Dr. Lance B. Eliot, MBA, PhD

<u>Chapter Title</u>

1 Eliot Framework for AI Self-Driving Cars

2 Versioning and Self-Driving Cars

3 Towing and Self-Driving Cars

4 Driving Styles and Self-Driving Cars

5 Bicyclists and Self-Driving Vehicles

6 Back-up Cams and Self-Driving Cars

7 Traffic Mix and Self-Driving Cars

8 Hot-Car Deaths and Self-Driving Cars

9 Machine Learning Performance and Self-Driving Cars

10 Sensory Illusions and Self-Driving Cars

11 Federated Machine Learning and Self-Driving Cars

12 Irreproducibility and Self-Driving Cars

13 In-Car Deliveries and Self-Driving Cars

This title is available via Amazon and other book sellers

<u>Companion Book By This Author</u>

Top Trends in
AI Self-Driving Cars

by Dr. Lance B. Eliot, MBA, PhD

<u>Chapter Title</u>

1 Eliot Framework for AI Self-Driving Cars

2 Responsibility and Self-Driving Cars

3 Changing Lanes and Self-Driving Cars

4 Procrastination and Self-Driving Cars

5 NTSB Report and Tesla Car Crash

6 Start Over AI and Self-Driving Cars

7 Freezing Robot Problem and Self-Driving Cars

8 Canarying and Self-Driving Cars

9 Nighttime Driving and Self-Driving Cars

10 Zombie-Cars Taxes and Self-Driving Cars

11 Traffic Lights and Self-Driving Cars

12 Reverse Engineering and Self-Driving Cars

13 Singularity AI and Self-Driving Cars

This title is available via Amazon and other book sellers

<u>Companion Book By This Author</u>

AI Innovations and Self-Driving Cars

by Dr. Lance B. Eliot, MBA, PhD

<u>Chapter Title</u>

1 Eliot Framework for AI Self-Driving Cars

2 API's and Self-Driving Cars

3 Egocentric Designs and Self-Driving Cars

4 Family Road Trip and Self-Driving Cars

5 AI Developer Burnout and Tesla Car Crash

6 Stealing Secrets About Self-Driving Cars

7 Affordability and Self-Driving Cars

8 Crossing the Rubicon and Self-Driving Cars

9 Addicted to Self-Driving Cars

10 Ultrasonic Harm and Self-Driving Cars

11 Accidents Contagion and Self-Driving Cars

12 Non-Stop 24x7 and Self-Driving Cars

13 Human Life Spans and Self-Driving Cars

This title is available via Amazon and other book sellers

Companion Book By This Author

Crucial Advances for
AI Self-Driving Cars

by Dr. Lance B. Eliot, MBA, PhD

Chapter Title

1 Eliot Framework for AI Self-Driving Cars

2 Ensemble Learning and AI Self-Driving Cars

3 Ghost in AI Self-Driving Cars

4 Public Shaming of AI Self-Driving

5 Internet of Things (IoT) and AI Self-Driving Cars

6 Personal Rapid Transit (RPT) and Self-Driving Cars

7 Eventual Consistency and AI Self-Driving Cars

8 Mass Transit Future and AI Self-Driving Cars

9 Coopetition and AI Self-Driving Cars

10 Electric Vehicles (EVs) and AI Self-Driving Cars

11 Dangers of In-Motion AI Self-Driving Cars

12 Sports Cars and AI Self-Driving Cars

13 Game Theory and AI Self-Driving Cars

This title is available via Amazon and other book sellers

ABOUT THE AUTHOR

Dr. Lance B. Eliot, MBA, PhD is the CEO of Techbruim, Inc. and Executive Director of the Cybernetic Self-Driving Car Institute, and has over twenty years of industry experience including serving as a corporate officer in a billion dollar firm and was a partner in a major executive services firm. He is also a serial entrepreneur having founded, ran, and sold several high-tech related businesses. He previously hosted the popular radio show *Technotrends* that was also available on American Airlines flights via their in-flight audio program. Author or co-author of a dozen books and over 400 articles, he has made appearances on CNN, and has been a frequent speaker at industry conferences.

A former professor at the University of Southern California (USC), he founded and led an innovative research lab on Artificial Intelligence in Business. Known as the "AI Insider" his writings on AI advances and trends has been widely read and cited. He also previously served on the faculty of the University of California Los Angeles (UCLA), and was a visiting professor at other major universities. He was elected to the International Board of the Society for Information Management (SIM), a prestigious association of over 3,000 high-tech executives worldwide.

He has performed extensive community service, including serving as Senior Science Adviser to the Vice Chair of the Congressional Committee on Science & Technology. He has served on the Board of the OC Science & Engineering Fair (OCSEF), where he is also has been a Grand Sweepstakes judge, and likewise served as a judge for the Intel International SEF (ISEF). He served as the Vice Chair of the Association for Computing Machinery (ACM) Chapter, a prestigious association of computer scientists. Dr. Eliot has been a shark tank judge for the USC Mark Stevens Center for Innovation on start-up pitch competitions, and served as a mentor for several incubators and accelerators in Silicon Valley and Silicon Beach. He served on several Boards and Committees at USC, including having served on the Marshall Alumni Association (MAA) Board in Southern California.

Dr. Eliot holds a PhD from USC, MBA, and Bachelor's in Computer Science, and earned the CDP, CCP, CSP, CDE, and CISA certifications. Born and raised in Southern California, and having traveled and lived internationally, he enjoys scuba diving, surfing, and sailing.

ADDENDUM

Sociotechnical Insights and AI Driverless Cars

Practical Advances in Artificial Intelligence (AI) and Machine Learning

By

Dr. Lance B. Eliot, MBA, PhD

———

For supplemental materials of this book, visit:

www.ai-selfdriving-cars.guru

For special orders of this book, contact:

LBE Press Publishing

Email: LBE.Press.Publishing@gmail.com

www.ingramcontent.com/pod-product-compliance
Lightning Source LLC
Chambersburg PA
CBHW051230050326
40689CB00007B/862